THE
SPLENDOUR
OF AFRICA

DON CARL STEFFEN

WITH PHOTOGRAPHS BY THE AUTHOR

WALKER AND COMPANY NEW YORK

THE SPLENDOUR OF AFRICA

to the tenth legion

Contents

Prologue

The siren call of Africa has enticed man at least since the beginning of recorded history. Traders, slavers, geographers, historians, adventurers, explorers, kings and emperors, from Indonesia, China, India, Persia, Arabia, Europe and America have felt the lure, the fascination. Armies of great conquerors, Alexander, Caesar, Napoleon, have trod there. A legion of writers and poets have succumbed to her charms. Some of the greatest land and sea sagas of world exploration responded to her inscrutable challenge.

Although man poked ineffectually at the flanks of Africa for centuries, she remained the Dark Continent, scorching the curious moths with her black flame. Thousands of lives—black as well as white—have been claimed by Africa as the price for yielding her secrets. Only in the nineteenth century were a dare-devil few permitted to wrest open the doors to her unknown reaches—and the splendors they saw there were incredible, so far beyond the ken of man's experience on the rest of this planet that the courageous discoverers of these tales were ridiculed as clumsy prevaricators, unworthy Baron Munchausens. Even less than a hundred years ago, maps of Africa were detailed only on the fringes, the interior left blank, or labeled "unknown."

Today the Dark Continent is dark no more. The blank spaces are inked in. Africa's physical secrets are known. Her barren deserts, snow-capped peaks, mighty rivers and shrouded jungles are tracked, open to all—both men and women. Even her human achievements, so long hidden through lack of written languages, are emerging, are being explored by new methods. Fossils of the oldest man known have been found there. Ancient arts, kingdoms and wisdoms are being unearthed. The sterile theories of African racial inferiority used to justify slavery—which spread Africans more widely across the globe than any people but the Europeans—have disintegrated. Black Africa, the former Dark Continent, eagerly strides from the Stone and Iron Ages into today and tomorrow.

The giants of exploration have faded from the African scene, but the splendors they discovered are still there—the lands, the peoples, the animals, the skies—and now are easily accessible to today's explorer. Air links to other continents and among African cities and towns are extensive. Automobile rental agencies operate in all major cities, and roads, if rough, are plentiful. Hotels, many of them air-conditioned, are found tucked in all corners of the continent, serving healthful, palatable food and pure water. Safaris with their lines of porters, months of travel, and many discomforts and dangers are available but no longer necessary, and a visit to great game herds or Stone Age villages is a matter of a few hours, rather than days.

Modern Africa is more than animals and tribes, as proud shepherds of new independence so justly vaunt. However, it is the call of ancient Africa, that African heritage of antiquity, mystery and the exotic, that mesmerizes today as yesterday. It is this primeval pull that twists the belly of every boy, young or old. It was this mystical attraction that enabled Edgar Rice Burroughs—who never saw Africa—to hitch the armchairs of millions to the vine that swung Tarzan forever into the lore of Africa.

That Africa exists still. Come, she awaits you.

ETHIOPIA

A proud race, the Ethiopians. Independent for over three thousand years, they claim the most illustrious of ancestors: no less than King Solomon and the Queen of Sheba.

The legend has it that a dying King of Ethiopia named his daughter Makeda as successor, and she was crowned Queen of Sheba, ruler of the Ethiopian empire. An Ethiopian trader, having delivered rare woods and jewels for King Solomon's temple, returned with a vivid tale of the luxury of Solomon's court. Intrigued, the Queen organized a caravan of seven hundred and ninety-seven camels to visit Jerusalem.

It was a case of love at first sight—she with his wisdom and riches, he with her singular beauty. A virgin, she refused his urgent pleas to bear him a child. But Solomon's reputation for wisdom was well merited. To mark the end of her visit, he ordered a great feast, at which all foods served were heavily spiced and salted. As the feast ended late, he offered her a bed in his quarters, which she accepted only after he promised to respect her virginity. He in turn demanded her surprised promise to take nothing from the palace that was not hers—or he would take her.

That night a slim hand pushed by a raging thirst raised a cool jug of water to hot lips, and Solomon's snare closed. To protests that it was only water she was taking, Solomon answered that water was the most precious substance in his kingdom. A royal descendant has written, "The legend does not tell whether the Queen of Sheba enjoyed paying the price of her indiscretion; suffice it to say she paid."

The legend continues that a son was born of this mutual thirst, Menelik, who visited his father in Jerusalem. Solomon recognized Menelik as his first-born son, and decreeing that only Menelik's male heirs were to rule Ethiopia, he sent back with him as his servants all the first-born sons of his own officers and counselors.

Today, Emperor Haile Selassie claims direct lineage from Menelik, and one of his principal titles is "Conquering Lion of the Tribe of Judah." The black Jews of Ethiopia, the Falashas, who practice an archaic type of Judaism, claim descent from the first-born sons, as do several noble Ethiopian families. The Imperial Coat of Arms of Christian Ethiopia consists of a combination of the Christian Cross and the Jewish Star of David.

Proof? The legend is too time-shrouded for either supporters or detractors to unravel. Indisputable, however, is that Ethiopia has always been a physical and spiritual crossroads, the link between Black Africa and the Middle East. A thousand years before Christ, tribes from the Arabian peninsula crossed the Red Sea and intermarried with the native Hamitic people, giving them a Semitic culture. Further blending came with the incursions of Negro tribes from the upper Nile. The conversion of the royal family to Christianity in the fourth century, and the Moslem raids in the eighth century, recast the native animist religions.

Ethiopia's strategic position, with its coast on the Red Sea, its control of one of the sources of the Nile, and rumors of its vast gold mines and riches, has been the cause of belligerent envy since the beginning of history. In spite of repeated invasions, no conquest, not even that of Mussolini, has been permanent, although each successive influx has left behind its stamp of language, customs and blood. Constant warfare and incessant local power struggles forced the various kings to be warrior chieftains, and its common citizens to be fighting men. This tradition was upheld by the Ethiopians in the Korean War, where they achieved an enviable renown, never leaving their wounded or dead on the battlefield. Today's "typical" Ethiopian is a proud man, seemingly without complexes—either superior or inferior—ranging in color from light tan to blue-black ebony, handsome and of a regal carriage in movement.

Because of the fierce nature of these people, their constant struggles and their harsh natural environment, terrible punishments were once common in Ethiopia. Offenders, even such figures as judges and counselors who had incurred the wrath of a king, were frequently flogged, tied to a stake and beaten with whips that cut to the bone. Defeated enemies risked having their eyes ripped out, or their right arm and left leg torn off, or other mutilations.

Those convicted of treason were not buried, but were thrown in the streets, left to the hyenas at night—the rising sun revealing partially eaten bodies in the gutters.

Some of this ferocity exists even today, although thoroughly condemned and punished by the Government. Among certain Danakil desert tribesmen, the ancient practice persists of requiring a prospective bridegroom to present to his future father-in-law, as a proof of his manhood, the freshly severed testicles of an enemy. Another custom, albeit rather infrequent, is that of cutting a steak from a live cow; the wound is then bandaged with a poultice of mud and manure, the hide pinned back in place with thorns, the steak eaten raw.

It was this story more than any other of his improbable tales that brought the eighteenth-century explorer James Bruce the scorn and abuse of his fellow Englishmen, eventually causing him to retire to his estates in a vast sulk. Bruce had married a wealthy wine merchant's daughter, studied Arabic at the Escorial in Spain and Ethiopian from Ludolf's writings, then retired from the family business at thirty-one to seek the source of the Blue Nile. A mystery had confounded and intrigued for centuries every observer of the Nile: in the heat of Egyptian summer the river swept in flood through—and seemingly out of—a waterless desert. Arranging to be appointed Consul-General in Algiers, he explored the north coast of Africa and the Arabian peninsula, and arrived in Massawa on the Red Sea coast in 1769. He penetrated to Axum and Gondar, the seats of Ethiopian power, where he became a valuable if suspect member of the King's entourage, eventually going to battle with the King's troops, hiding his white skin with a black silk scarf. The presence of this six-foot-five-inch Scottish giant in the King's troop was remembered long after he had left the country.

Bruce did discover the ultimate source of the Blue Nile, and he even followed the Nile down through Egypt, escaping royal tantrums after falling from favor. He was one of the few lucky travelers in medieval Ethiopia. Others, such as Portuguese, French and British travelers, missionaries and diplomats, were detained for years—as many as thirty or forty in some cases—or were executed out of hand.

The Twentieth Century's traveler has it better. Instead of taking six months or a year to reach the heart of Ethiopia, an overnight flight from Europe suffices.

Arriving over Ethiopia at dawn, the first glimpse of this corner of Africa for today's traveler will probably be the sun off the eight-thousand-foot escarpment and across the Danakil desert, rocketing out of the Red Sea, seeming to rise so fast that the first new minutes see it already well on its way to the evening horizon. Its light, coming at first from below, changes from the dust-and-sand-red of morning's horizontal rays to the pale gold that pulls morning mist from the ground and promises the white heat of noon. Shadows a hundred miles long shorten with greyhound speed as the peaks, mesas and ambas lose their advantage to the sun's ascending course. The black rivers of shadow drowned in the jigsaw gorges of Ethiopia's highlands slowly dry up as the sunbeams probe the still depths.

Ethiopia is a great plateau rising seven to nine thousand feet from the sea. Like much of Africa, Ethiopia is blessed and damned with monsoon rains, intense tropical deluges, almost daily from June to mid-September. And this water must go somewhere; as it seeks the sea, it continues its now million-year-old task of ripping and gouging out its canyon highways through the rich Ethiopian soil. The entire highland is crisscrossed by gorges, the floors of some of them four to five thousand feet lower than the mesa itself, all carrying the life-giving silt two thousand seven hundred and fifty miles down through the western desert to the thin green line through the sterile sand that is Egypt, renewing the Nile Valley fertility by countless annual floods—truly the lifeblood of Egypt.

This dependence of Egypt on the rains and soil of Ethiopia was early recognized by Egyptian and Ethiopian statesmen. One chronicler writes that in A.D. 1093 the Nile failed to rise; the Caliph sent gifts to the King of Ethiopia, and the Nile flooded. Two hundred years later an Ethiopian king actually started to divert Ethiopian waters to the east so as to dry up Egypt. Rumors of attempts to poison the waters of the Nile as they left Lake Tana in order to subdue the Moslems of Egypt gained credence hundreds of years ago. Even today, with the coming completion of the dam at Aswan, there is a great engineering problem of how to keep the silt from filling the dam—and Egypt's rulers are faced with the pressing problem of generating a chemical fertilizer industry to replace the annual soil replenishment downstream from the blocking Aswan dam complex.

The source of the Blue Nile, Lake Tana, is itself three thousand feet lower than the surrounding plateau. The thousand square miles of water is dotted with islands, many of which have been holy refuges since monks took shelter there from the onslaught of pagan tribes, soon after the conversion of the country to Coptic Christianity in the fourth century, and from the Moslems four hundred years later. Even today many of the islands and juniper-shrouded monasteries are religious centers, and absolutely forbidden to the defiling foot of woman.

The entire country is replete with churches and monasteries, even though thousands of them were sacked and destroyed several times by the invading Moslems. These relics attest to the religious zeal and immense wealth of the kings of Ethiopia. While having only the expense of supporting themselves and immediate families, the kings collected tribute from governors and rulers all over the country. The Portuguese Alvarez wrote of one tribute he saw being paid in 1520, in which three thousand horses, three thousand mules, six thousand bearers and three men bearing gold took ten days to pass before the King in the tribute procession. With wealth of this fantastic degree, the kings could and did make frequent large contributions of new churches and monasteries, and gold, silks, paintings and other precious furnishings. Much of this wealth was destroyed or carried off by sacking Moslems, but the churches are still filled with priceless illuminated manuscripts, paintings and precious metalwork. Some of the most interesting are on these Lake Tana island refuges.

Even the canoes on Lake Tana are Biblical—bundles of papyrus rushes tied together, plying the lake as ferries and fishing boats. The lake is rich in fish, and when the fruit of the low-hanging trees on the shores is ripe, fish can be literally scooped up as they mass to snap up berries knocked into the water by the clouds of feeding birds.

But the water itself is treacherous. Like most water in Africa, it is infected by a parasite, which lives first in a snail host and next in a human, causing the disease of bilharzia, or schistosomiasis, a debilitating infection weakening 80 per cent of the people of the Nile River system, and caught by mere contact with sluggish water.

The overflow of Lake Tana, the outlet at Chara-chara where the Nile starts its voyage to the Mediterranean, is a distinct disappointment. It should be a crushing cataract, an experience equal to the majesty of the Nile, but it is hardly a falls—just a ripple, a gentle sliding away of excess water from the placid Tana basin. This disillusioning peace and serenity is devastatingly destroyed in less than twenty miles. Struggling through two miles of bush, crossing the Nile once via a partially ruined but delicate multi-arched Portuguese bridge—the Portuguese seem to have been first everywhere in Africa—one emerges from the trees onto the headland face to face with the cataract of the Blue Nile Falls, awed by the stark power and savagery. The Nile approaches the Falls in a valley-wide torrent, sweeping over the precipice in three great plunges—with a series of thread-like waterfalls chuting down in between—to strike the fall pool at one's feet with a dull, shuddering roar. Mist spins up higher than the Falls, whipping from side to side with the wind, now veiling, now revealing the Falls, finally descending rainbow-arched to the lush headlands in an everlasting spray of rain. "Tisisat," "Smoke of Fire," the Ethiopians appropriately name the Falls. Like the magic of a campfire, Tisisat draws and holds the eye, sweeps one up and sears the soul with man's ineffectual size. Long moments pass before the soaking "rain" pushes one reluctantly back away from the sight through the trees.

Flowing southeast out of Lake Tana, the Blue Nile hurtles the Falls and races through its long loop of gorge to the northwest, where it leaves the mountains for the desert and joins the White Nile. This carved chasm separates world from world. In the past it effectively stopped any meaningful travel or communication between two large sections of the country. Today it still separates the world on the mesa from that of the canyon floor. On top, a moderate, nearly temperate climate, relatively healthful and free of disease, supports a population of farmers growing temperate and sub-tropical crops, and herders with their heavy-humped, turkey-gulleted zebu cattle. On the gorge's floor—in places requiring a day to climb down the three or four thousand feet—it is the tropics, the jungle. Temperatures soar, the air is humid and oppressive, malaria abounds, crops are true torrid zone plants, fish from the Nile is a staple and the people themselves are of another day, some of them having even kept the language of the original Hamitic inhabitants of Ethiopia. Only recently with the aid of helicopters has exploration of the gorge been undertaken. No one has ever followed the river through the chasm. An American adventurer carried specially constructed boats to Lake Tana, only to have them smashed in the first few moments after launching.

Across Lake Tana from the Blue Nile outlet, in the foothills a few miles from the shore, lies Gondar, "Home of Kings." It was the capital for Ethiopian kings from 1632, when Fasilidas chose it, until the late nineteenth century, when Menelik II founded the present capital, Addis Ababa.

Half a dozen castles still stand in the walled royal enclosure, dominated by Fasilidas' castle, a five-storied, four-towered building, with the great hall one hundred and twenty feet long, and filled with high-vaulted rooms once decorated with hand-carved ceilings, walls of Venetian mirror, and wainscoting of ivory.

Partially destroyed and rebuilt many times, the last restoration done by the Italian invaders in the thirties, the martial excitement and splendor of the regal age still permeate the air. One feels the Emperor and his retinue could be absent on one of the frequent raids, and that they might return soon. Indeed Gondar was practically empty for long periods of time when it was the royal capital. Continual

campaigns against rebels and invaders frequently took the Emperor, his government and his army away from Gondar.

But whether on the march or in Gondar, the same ceremonies and customs were observed. When moving in state, the imperial procession was headed by six horses and six mules, saddled and each led by four grooms. They were followed by a large group of pages, usually Moslem or pagan boys captured as children, since they would have loyalty only to their royal master. The imperial pride of lions, ever-present symbol of imperial power, stalked next, each lion restrained by heavy chains held by men on either side. Then the Emperor, mounted on a white mule led by six pages, and shielded from common eyes by a moving wall of curtains suspended from poles held by pages. He was followed by a hundred men bearing urns of meat, and another hundred carrying baskets of bread. The nobles and the thousands of commoners took the rear.

On a campaign, the column could be an astounding affair. Everyone went along. A hundred thousand warriors, servants, slaves, women and children marched twenty or thirty miles a day. Great flocks of sheep and herds of cattle and tons of baggage straggled across the gorges and plateaux of Ethiopia.

At night, a plethora of tents for the two churches with their portable altars, the bakery for communion bread, the Emperor's treasure, the queen, the bishop and other thousands of the twenty thousand necessary for housing were pitched long before the tail of this great snail inched into camp.

Normally, the Emperor was shielded from all eyes except those of his court, the bishop and priests, the nobles, and during a campaign, his war chiefs. During the time of the Portuguese missionaries, this had been changed so that His Majesty was unveiled to his people from a high platform on Christmas, Easter and Holy Cross day, a privilege granted to still discontent when the court had concealed King Alexander's death more than three years while gorging themselves on the tribute delivered to the dead king.

But the evening feast, whether on the march or in the capital, and especially when a victory could be celebrated, could turn into a drunken orgy. With the court assembled, the Emperor had no need of veils, and partook as heartily as any of his courtiers.

For these feasts the first of many steers was pummeled into the dining hall or tent and securely tied. Knives flashed, blood spurted and living steaks were devoured to the wail of the animal's anguish. As Bruce wrote, "The prodigious noise the animal makes is a signal for the company to sit down to table." Servants scurried under booted encouragement to replenish rapidly dwindling mountains of injera, berbere and wat. Casks of tej were trundled in and broached with a war ax—treacherous mead of honey warmed already heated bodies. The bloody skeleton was thrown out to feed slaves, and another balking, bawling beast was hurried to the impatient diners.

Appetites were unfettered, nothing was denied the virile conquerors. "Love lights all its fires," Bruce wrote, "and everything is permitted with absolute freedom. There is no coyness, no delays, no need of appointments or retirement to gratify their wishes: there are no rooms but one, in which they sacrifice both to Bacchus and Venus." A sudden two-seat vacancy at the long table. Those nearest would stand to offer their cloaks as shield, as Bacchus made way for Venus. Gorging guests continued, listening without opprobrium or smirks as achievement was advertised with a keening heartiness that surmounted the general roar. Bruce says, "They seem to think it as great a shame to make love in silence as to eat so." Another cask was breached, another steer was stabbed, other cloaks, other bodies were pressed into service. And, "All this passes without remark or scandal, not a licentious word is uttered, nor the most distant joke upon the transaction." Couple succeeded couple till, finally, Venus, surfeited, slumbered.

If the feast were in Gondar, the morrow was automatically spent at the royal baths, the Baths of Fasilidas, still standing, a basalt block building with its adjoining pool so perfect for dispelling the ravages of drink and gluttony. There would also be a procession to one of the churches for the royal communion, probably the still standing Debre Berhan, slightly resembling the Parthenon of

Athens, with its columns and porches on four sides, and a treasure of early handwritten versions of the Bible and wall paintings, or perhaps to the church at Gorgora, built by the Jesuit Pedro Paez on the shores of Lake Tana. Ethiopian churches today, especially in the countryside, are practically unchanged since those days. A circular thatched hut forty feet in height, forty feet in diameter is the first wall of the church—a replaceable protection against the rains. Inside, dry cut grass carpets the floor. A second, circular, dried mud wall blocks the way. Stooping through low, arched minuscule openings, one discovers the church itself, an ancient vaulted stone edifice, square and separate from the outer thatched roof. The church door proper is barred by a threadbare tapestry, for only the priests are allowed to enter. Women are excluded from the entire church area. Black priests lift gauze coverings from medieval icons depicting Christ on the crucifix surrounded by His mother and the Apostles—all white—with black devils here and there. Drums and trumpets furnish music.

The most spectacular highway in Africa winds the two hundred and forty miles from Gondar to Axum. From the level of Lake Tana the road mounts laboriously to the level of the high plateau, then drops dizzyingly in endless switchbacks and hairpin turns to the Takazze River, over three thousand feet below.

The Takazze, downstream known as the Atbara, is one of the principal tributaries of the Nile, and is a powerful, eroding river. Indeed, the British invasion of 1868, rescuing their Ambassador and Special Envoy, lost more men in the return crossing of the Takazze than it did in storming and taking the Ethiopian stronghold; and it was in this area that several of the artillery elephants laid down and refused to continue, forcing their destruction.

It is claimed that this Takazze gorge is large enough to "lose" the Grand Canyon of the Colorado in its depths. From the rim, looking out over the miles and miles of void, one does not doubt it. A tangled, twisted, tumultuous mass of indescribable moon scenery reflects the hammering power of drop upon drop of water.

But somehow the harshness is soft—puzzling, till it

slowly dawns that, in contrast to the denuded and rainbow-hued rock of the American Grand Canyon, here everything is swathed in a soft spring-green growth of vegetation, with only an occasional outcrop of bare rock.

During the birth of this land, when subterranean volcanic turbulence thrust the extensive alluvial deposits to mesa height, immense cores of molten granite shot through these soft deposits. As millenniums of monsoons washed the soft sedentary formations of the mesa down to Egypt and the sea, these tough volcanic cores were little affected. They resist today, cluttering the gorge and sculpturing the horizon as cones, needles, free-form trapezoids and ambas.

Ambas, the flat-topped peaks—really truncated cones or mesas, with often several square miles of land on top and rearing a thousand feet above the surrounding area—have cut into Ethiopian history nearly as much as they do into Takazze's profile. With perpendicular slopes, and minimal access easily defensible against a storming army by only a handful of men, they have served as last refuge for rebels resisting royal power, or as bastions for the Emperor in time of invasion. Debre Damos, an amba crowned with a medieval monastery, has proved impregnable in numerous sieges through the centuries mainly because it is necessary to climb a sixty-foot rope to reach even the first foothold in the tortuous ascent.

Ambas were also used as royal prisons. Once an emperor was crowned, all male relatives, except for his sons and their families, were imprisoned on an amba. They were accompanied by their families, were showered with lavish gifts from the Emperor, wanted for no physical comfort or need, but were held incommunicado, their freedom strictly limited to living and dying on the amba.

Only if the direct royal blood line expired would one of them be summoned to assume the crown. One such man, John, son of Jesus the Great, was chosen to replace a murdered king when he was seventy years old. Ironically he was poisoned a few months later and his son, Takla Hyamanot, was crowned, the king whom Bruce met upon his arrival.

The road the other side of Takazze mounts through

a tree-dotted savannah, then up the dizzying wall to the mesa and Axum, legendary capital of the Queen of Sheba and her son Menelik, a flourishing capital long before the birth of Christ. The *Periplus of the Erythraean Sea,* written in the first century A.D., describes it as a rich city, eight days march from the Red Sea, and the collection point for all ivory from beyond the Nile for shipment to the Roman Empire. Axum was influenced greatly by the Greek city-states. Its kings had Greek education; many official documents, letters and books were written in Greek; and coins were struck bearing inscriptions in Greek. Even today these copper coins wash out of the ground or are dug up by small boys at Axum and sold to tourists at a few pennies each.

It was the Axum King Ezana, obliterator of the great Nile civilization of Meroe, who was converted to Christianity in the middle of the fourth century. His conversion came about curiously. A Syrian trading ship put in for water on the Red Sea coast, and Ethiopians slaughtered all on the ship save two Christian boys, Aedesius and Frumentius, who were presented to the King. Frumentius as time went by converted Ezana, and later became the first Bishop of Axum.

In the sixth century, Julian, an ambassador of the Emperor Justinian, described the Emperor at Axum. He rode in a four-wheeled, gold-plated coach, drawn by four elephants, carried a gold shield and two small golden spears, and was naked except for a brief linen breech-clout and a linen, gold-embroidered turban. A golden collar, golden bracelets and a crisscross of leather chest straps encrusted with pearls decorated his powerful black body. A resplendent figure.

These Axum emperors subdued and ruled territories stretching from the Arab peninsula to Nubia. Strangely enough, in view of their eventual withdrawal from the world—as Gibbon says, they "slept near a thousand years, forgetful of the world, by whom they were forgotten"— the Ethiopians at that time were accomplished sailors and piratical scourges of the sea, even sacking Jidda, the port of Mecca, in 702.

Legend has it that when Mohammed announced his evangelical mission only the Ethiopian king answered with encouragement, and sheltered Moslem refugees from the pagan rulers of Mecca. Mohammed is supposed to have said, "Avoid the Abyssinians as long as they avoid you." But the sacking of Jidda raised the specter of Christian Ethiopians plundering the holy city of Mecca. Moslems occupied the Red Sea ports of Ethiopia, and desultory warfare followed for centuries. In spite of this, as late as the tenth century Arab historians wrote that there was no *jihad*, or holy war, against the Ethiopians.

But in the sixteenth century the full fury of the Moslems fell on Ethiopia. Led by Ahmed the Gran, or left-handed, and spearheaded by two hundred Turkish musketeers, the Moslems raged through the King's army, which was superior in numbers but had no firearms. Axum and other strongholds were systematically destroyed, the churches pillaged and burned, and the kingdom's accumulated wealth of centuries carried away. The amba serving as the royal prison was taken, and all the princes put to the sword. Ethiopian writers record that nine out of ten persons were forced to embrace the Moslem faith.

Only King Lebna Dengel with a small force escaped into the mountains. Eight years passed before he managed to smuggle a messenger out to the King of Portugal for aid; six years later the Portuguese landed four hundred riflemen, under Vasco da Gama's son, Christopher. Lebna Dengel had died and his son Claudius was now King, but the Moslems had been unable to capture the small band to complete the regicide.

After several inconclusive battles with the Portuguese, Ahmed the Gran secured an additional nine hundred Turkish matchlocks, and killed half the Portuguese, including Christopher da Gama. The remaining Portuguese, joined by King Claudius and his band, retreated to an impregnable amba and rearmed themselves from an arms cache previously hidden by da Gama. Their chemist made gunpowder from sulphur and saltpeter found locally. Ethiopians rallied to their king until there was a force of eight thousand foot and five hundred horse soldiers, and this

resurrected army fell upon an astounded Ahmed the Gran near Lake Tana. Ahmed was killed and his demoralized army scattered, except for the Turks, who fought on to the end, only forty managing to escape. This defeat curbed the threat of Moslem domination of Ethiopia, but the cultural heritage of that occupation lingers on; between a third and a half of Ethiopia is still Moslem.

Axum, in ruins, was abandoned as capital, and gradually dissolved into the sleepy life of the hinterland. But the skeleton of the Axum that had been remained. Before the conversion to Christianity, giant obelisks or steles had been erected, either as funerary monuments to kings or to some dark god. Their purpose is unknown. Bruce saw forty such steles in the eighteenth century. Many were toppled by the Moslem invaders, others by earthquakes, one was taken to Rome during the Italian occupation. Some still stand, and others are being raised again.

The largest, a stele of over one hundred and thirty feet, surpasses by far the tallest Egyptian obelisk. Although very probably of similar inspiration, the Axum steles are uniquely different. They are rectangular, rather than square, and the peak is carved with an oval crescent and disk, possibly a symbol of Mahrem, the Ethiopian god of war—as against the pyramidal point of the Egyptian monuments. Also, they are uninscribed, thus relegating any modern guesses as to their *raison d'être* to mere speculation. They are, however, heavily carved, quite obviously in imitation of a dwelling, with a door at ground level, then log floors, upper-story windows, more floors, rising to the capping religious symbol. Perhaps they represent the various levels of heaven, or of hell.

Not only why these steles were created but how they were raised—the sheer engineering problem—is a mystery. They were raised at least sixteen centuries ago by a primitive people. In 1964, the United States Air Force, using some of the most powerful cranes available today, was defeated in the task of raising even the broken sections of the largest stele. It couldn't be done. The stele still lies there.

A hundred yards from the steles is the church of Mary of Zion, constructed on a spot already considered holy in the pre-Christian era, destroyed by Ahmed Gran, and rebuilt in its present rectangular form in the seventeenth century by Portuguese artisans. In the church's courtyard four pillars and a stone throne—dating from the pagan era—mark the site where all Ethiopian emperors were enthroned and crowned until Menelik II founded Addis Ababa.

A Portuguese missionary described the coronation ceremony at Axum. The procession moved in cadenced step toward the cathedral, halting before a silk ribbon, held across the way by virgins of noble blood. "Who are you?" they asked. "I am King of Israel." They refused passage; the same question and answer resulted in another refusal. The third time, the King answered, "I am King of Zion," and slashed the ribbon with his sword. The maidens gave way, "You are truly our King of Zion." The procession moved toward the cathedral amid a bedlam of applause, drums, trumpets and gunfire, the King was crowned and the ceremony ended with a mass in the cathedral at which the King took communion.

The crowns of many of these kings, including the coronation crown of the present Emperor, Haile Selassie I, are guarded by priests at the cathedral of Mary of Zion in Axum. Made of gold and silver, and studded with diamonds, rubies, emeralds and other precious stones, they, and a collection of illuminated manuscripts and gold and painted crosses, will be displayed at the new cathedral nearby, expected to be completed during 1965.

Today the capital is Addis Ababa, to the south, far from the medieval scenes of Gondar and Axum, though the exotic is still part of imperial life. The Emperor's palace is a gem of Oriental-African splendor, richly furnished, filled with ancient and artistic treasures. The imperial pride of lions is today still omnipresent, the savage symbol of absolute power, preceding the Emperor in state. One can even pet—if intestinal fortitude is up to the test—a brute of a black-maned lion, Tojo, as he paces ceaselessly in the imperial gardens at the end of his chain leash.

Across the avenue from the palace, perched on a hill, sits Africa Hall, headquarters of the Organization of African Unity, with its sweeping modern lines and great stained-glass scenes of Ethiopian life done in the tradition of the medieval workers of illuminated manuscripts. Farther up the mountain slope lies Trinity Cathedral, with its altar kept inviolate from the eyes of disbelievers.

But the heart of Addis Ababa is the market: acres and acres of Ethiopians, hawking, shopping, haggling, objecting, laughing, gaining, losing, buying, selling. A kaleidoscope of life.

A rainbow of Ethiopians: Amharas, dominant plateau Ethiopians, tall, aquiline, disdainful of the crush, princely in bearing; Gallas, round-faced, very dark, nomadically independent; Tigreans, only partly assimilated, instinctively aware of the linguistic and cultural heritage, more Arab than African; an occasional Danakil, warlike, desert nomad, uneasy in this mountain city, fiercely proud, contemptuously confident.

Especially on Saturday, every road, every trail streams steadily with traffic to the market, wares loaded on donkeys, mules, horses, even a few camels, but mostly on Ethiopian heads. The loads carried stagger the credulity of a Westerner—logs thirty feet long that cannot weigh less than four hundred pounds, hand-hammered metalware one piece inside the other rising fifteen feet over the bearer's head, cages of chickens, packs of skins, great mounds of injera (the local bread relished with such gusto when sprinkled with berbere pepper nearly impossible for other throats and stomachs to accept), ingeniously balanced pyramids of earthenware, cloth, utensils.

The traveler buys Oriental spices, fluorescent silks, a sword, silver-studded muskets, a leopard skin, a lump of gold, has a garment sewn by the male seamstresses, listens to the storytellers, selects a Coptic pectoral cross, or sifts the piles of Austrian Maria Theresa silver dollars. Half a million of these were struck under special contract with the Austrian treasury for use during the 1868 British invasion—for decades this was the only acceptable currency in Ethiopia, and not just any Maria Theresa dollar, but only the minting of 1780, which shows a vast expanse of the regal bust.

Anything might be found in this Babel of a market; the search is its own reward.

KENYA/
TANGANYIKA

East Africa seems to be one large zoo. Sharp eyes will pick out the herds of impala, zebra, water buffalo and wildebeest as the airliner comes in to land over the Nairobi Game Park.

Nairobi itself is a modern city of wide boulevards and handsome buildings, distinguishable as African only by the wide variety of flowers. It is laced and splattered with every conceivable color, as the purple jacaranda trees vie with the blocks and blocks of bougainvillea, flame trees and dozens of other flowering African shrubs.

It is too modern and too comfortable for our vision of Africa. But only forty miles from the city the blacktop ends, and the baobab and fever trees begin. Here is the Africa of Hemingway and Ruark.

Two hours more and one reaches Mtito Andei gate, opening to the eight thousand square miles of Tsavo National Park, where Africa's prehistoric fauna still live, breed and die. But the age of the rugged explorer is dead; twentieth-century luxury has invaded the bush.

At a lodge in Tsavo such as Kilaguni, "Hill of the Rhino," the evening "sundowner" is no longer a room-temperature beer or a warm gin-and-tonic. It is one's favorite cocktail served with plenty of clear ice by an attentive waiter. One may have cooled off in the swimming pool before settling into a comfortable armchair on the ninety-foot veranda to watch the game at their own waterhole, a few yards away.

Even in the hottest part of the day one can see herds of zebra come and go, a hundred impala in small groups browsing, long Indian-files of guinea fowl racing to and fro as though they couldn't fly, and solitary wart hogs kneeling down to grub the red earth, while troops of baboons and monkeys sport throughout the area, even trying to pull down the electric wiring.

Over the entire scene flutters a variegated cloud of birds, from finches to buzzards, from ducks to hornbills, those slaves of instinct who mud up their mates in a tree hollow to hatch their offspring, then work themselves to a frazzle finding and pushing their mates' breakfasts in bed through the bill opening.

Beyond the waterhole, in the middle distance that is Tanganyika, a huge ridge slopes up into the clouds, then slopes down identically to the plain. A puzzling symmetry, till by chance one looks above the clouds and sees the rest—the looming, snow-crested volcanic cone of Mount Kilimanjaro.

The afternoon drifts by lazily; drinks, cameras, field glasses litter the tables, lizards scurry for crumbs, and the parade of animals continues before the armchair explorers. One dines on the veranda at the hour one chooses. A sign in the bar reads, "Animals are requested to remain silent whilst guests are drinking—and vice versa." But, especially during dinner, the animals sometimes forget, and monkeys swing up the six-foot protection wall to the veranda to climb table legs and beg.

Dusk falls quickly. Kilimanjaro is still a dazzling white in the dying sun when the plain below is already a deep velvet. The orange and peach of the sky and clouds turn cobalt blue, then black. Floodlights, "night suns," have been shining since the sun dipped. One, just fifteen yards from the verandah, illuminates the spring that feeds the waterhole.

A small bull elephant is already hanging his trunk into the spring, the baboons and monkeys have drifted off to find a protective thorn tree, and now the impala, so tail-waggingly gay under the sun, move off with hesitating step into the dangerous dusk. A thin line of zebras approach for a last drink, down-spring from the elephant—the elephant allows no other animal to drink at the same spot as he—and barely dip their muzzles, when there is an agonized scream from the far side of the waterhole, bringing the game-watchers to their feet. Death is near. Simba is feeding late, or a leopard is early. The line of zebras frantically vanishes. The elephant whirls toward the sound, flapping ears backward and forward in warning, doubling his trunk over his massive skull, pawing the ground in eloquent warning.

The night is silent. The spring gurgles and calls. Finally, he drinks, submerging a yard of his trunk into the spring, lifting his head till his trunk is higher than gleam-

ing tusks and mouth, and squirting into his distended jaws with the sound of a fire hose.

He whirls suddenly to face the dark. Two more elephants silently appear, a huge bull and a female. The big bull walks straight to the young bull and shoulders him aside. Ears flapping, but obviously too small for this fight, the young bull stalks to the other side of the spring, and all three suck and squirt noisily, drinking at least twenty gallons of water in half an hour.

A rhino snuffles dustily out of the darkness and lowers his muzzle into the water. As time passes he becomes a statue. A fourth elephant, a gray bull, walks into the light, and the first young bull blocks his path to the spring. He changes course, circles and drinks from the far side of the spring. The rhino moves off obliquely, seemingly vaporized as he leaves the full glare of the spotlight—his ponderous mass invisible because of his coloring—yet his horned shadow attests spectrally to his presence.

The four elephants whirl, shoulder to shoulder, ears flipped forward, weak eyes peering as with twitching nostrils they trail the rhino till even the eerie shadow dissolves into the black. The huge bull pays court to the female, and they sway off into the night for their thudding mating.

The first young bull turns to the gray bull and slowly backs him away from the spring. Realizing his limits, the gray bull leaves to drink at the dirtier water of the waterhole. With no serious enemy but man, these elephants challenge each other much like stiff-backed dogs on a street corner. Even their rumbled growls sound like snarling dogs.

Three shooting stars in as many minutes fall from the tipped Big Dipper over Kilimanjaro. The gray bull elephant sullenly leaves the waterhole for the darkness. The young bull still stands, a lonely figure, seeming to ponder whether to drink more or not, then dips trunk, and solemnly and deliberately moves off. He, like all the others, pauses at the light's perimeter, evidently adjusting his weak eyesight. In spite of tremendous size, no sound is heard when he walks.

One is suddenly aware of the presence of a small group

of rhinos that have materialized in the light. A mother and her calf drink thoroughly but rapidly, then disappear. Two heavy rhino bulls, shining almost silver-white under the lights from their roll-encrusted dust, drink, then turn towards each other. Less than a yard apart they lower their heavy horns, snort, stomp the mud and resolutely announce a brawl. One of them is obviously smaller, and discretion pushes him backwards slowly, grudgingly, the larger advancing on him at an equal pace. An elephant breaches the light circle; it may be the young bull, still resentful, still belligerent, looking for a bruising battle. He comes up behind the larger rhino. The confident advance of the rhino suddenly wavers, caught between the small rhino and the elephant. He turns part way, trying to look in two directions at once. After a deadlock of some minutes, the elephant moves off again. The rhinos, differences forgotten, wheel in diverging directions and are instantly swallowed by the black night. Even when spoiling for conflict, these mastodonic tons of death-dealing flesh hesitate, weigh their chances, before passing that fatal point of no return to pit their strength and lives against equally awesome foes.

The clearing is empty for a moment. A clacking announces a porcupine as he waddles to the pool. Before reaching water, he freezes. A roar rips apart the black night. Even the birds, silver in the searchlight, extending their bug-eating day by these "night suns," wing back to the trees and rest motionless. The porcupine waddles into the bush. The silence is stirred by the wind rising in the darkness, a wind that almost seems black, that must be the same wind that has blown over Africa since time began. Shivering, listening to its whine, death is palpable in the African night.

Dawn reveals another Africa, a warm Africa. Colors are as intense as fresh paint. Fever trees are that first-day-of-spring green, the cumulus the perfect white sheep of the poets, the earth iron-red, the dried grasses silver. Guides and landrovers deliver one to any animal ordered.

There he is. A big tusker, standing ten feet at the shoulder and reaching up another ten feet with trunk to

tear off a thorn tree branch. He disdainfully ignores the approaching vehicle and continues to rip down branches. Tiring of this snail's pace, he leans the underside of his heavy tusks against the tree, pushes—just weighs. It is so much easier to feed if the tree is flat on the ground. He may not succeed today—the roots are too young and too firmly entrenched—but he will have that tree someday, for he lives longer and grows stronger as the tree becomes more brittle. The entire park attests to his prowess. Only in the tornado belt of the United States can so many twisted, smashed, defoliated trees be seen in one area. The elephant is destroying his own favorite food, since the yellow fever tree is not replacing itself as fast as it is uprooted.

A little later a pair of eyes peer down from the sky. A seventeen-foot giraffe is browsing another thorn tree. Trimming only branches it can reach instead of destroying whole trees, it is he who is responsible for the almost clipped-lawn look of the underside of the umbrella-like thorn trees. A bizarre animal, awkwardly spreading his stilts to drink, running with a deceptively swift rocking-chair gait, he is gentle and curious, stretching that neck to gaze at intruders—one kick powerful enough to give the hyenas another lion carcass.

The impalas are everywhere, single gracefully horned bucks leading harems of up to sixty does. They are almost lazy as they graze. When frightened they seem to reach full speed instantly and soar in prodigious leaps over bushes and small trees. Wart hogs fill the brush, shyer than the impalas, suspended from their erect skinny tails as they flee, stopping at a distance to stare back over their ugly warts and curved tusks. These warts are only growths that protect their eyes in their kneeling and rooting.

The zebras are the clowns in their striped pajamas, constantly cavorting, racing and jostling each other. They always appear slickly healthy even in the poorest of grazing areas, and are probably the most numerous and least fearful of all Tsavo's inhabitants.

Half a dozen miles from Kilaguni Lodge, Mzima Springs gush forth with mill-race intensity from a pile of black lava boulders, the water cold and delicious. The pool fed by the springs is home to a dozen hippos, their pink nostrils breaking the pool's surface with snorts, sputters and loud groans. A glass-walled room sunk below the pool's surface enables one to see the iceberg seven-tenths of the hippos, swimming and even walking around, being "groomed" by a school of barbus fish that feast on parasites. A few crocodiles live in the pool, and according to one story, possibly apocryphal, a young boy who insisted on dipping his arms in the edge of the pool was last seen in the jaws of one of these saurian monsters. Monkeys abound in the trees around the pool, climbing down to beg crackers, bread and cookies, or even to thrust thieving paws into bags and pockets. The males of these vervet monkeys have bright red and blue sex organs, the color stimulating sexual response in the females.

The variety and number of animals existing in East Africa amazes one, especially since much of the country is semi-arid, rising to a plateau of ten thousand feet. Tsavo country is typical: hot, dusty, covered with scrub growth of all kinds, and a heavy sprinkling of thorn trees and the barrel-based, scraggle-branched baobab. Africans say that when God made Africa he tired of trying to make a graceful tree of the baobab and angrily thrust it in the ground upside down, so it grows with its roots in the air and its branches under ground.

A few miles away, beyond the Tanganyika border, the plateau gives way to the steady rise of the far-flung aprons of Kilimanjaro, clothed in lush green of banana and sisal, with swirling mists nearly always hiding the upper reaches. A colossal mountain, it dominates the entire countryside, easily visible on clear days from planes landing at Nairobi a hundred miles away. At nineteen thousand three hundred and forty feet, it is the highest single mountain in the world. For centuries native Africans have lived in its shadow, seen its gleaming white peaks, witnessed its spectacular electrical discharges from thunderhead to thunderhead, and heard the booming echoes rolling down to the plain below. That an animist god should roam this mountain is to be expected. Anyone would be awed.

Eerie, unlikely, it is as disquieting to see today as it was when early explorers brought back word of a mountain of snow on the equator. The chill is not all from the ice. Hemingway and the leopard slip into one's thoughts.

In the hotel perched halfway up the mountain, the heat and glow from the circular fireplace are welcome— if somewhat startling when one remembers the sweltering plateau is only a twenty-minute ride below.

Within view of Kilimanjaro, slashing down across Africa from the Red Sea to Nyasaland, cuts a continental fault, a three-thousand-mile-long depression, the Great Rift Valley. Its walls are escarpments difficult to pass, and its floor is two thousand to three thousand feet lower than the bounding plateaux. It is fifty miles wide in places and collects much of Africa's rains in its great string of lakes.

Just west of the Rift cuts Olduvai Gorge, where the earliest prehistoric traces of man, the six-hundred-thousand-year-old skull of "Nutcracker Man," Zinjanthropus Boisei, was unearthed by Dr. L.S.B. Leakey, along with remains of giant pigs, sheep with a horn spread of twelve feet, and short-necked giraffes with six-foot antlers.

Here lie the Serengeti plains, roamed by the world's largest remaining game herds, over a million animals in five thousand square miles. During the rains, there is water everywhere, and the animals are scattered. When the rains cease, they migrate to permanent water sources, first massing in the central plains, then plodding out in lines trailing for miles; they take hours to pass a given point. One may see a hundred thousand wildebeest in one herd. Zebras, thirty thousand or more, arriving at a river to water, may leave a dozen dead in the mud, trampled in the inexorable crush toward the water. In a few hours they graze grass four feet tall down to a stubble for a mile on each side of the river. The carnivora follow, forced to migrate with their food supply: lions in prides of forty or more, leopards, cheetahs, pulling down the stragglers, the lame, the aged. Then come hyenas in hundreds, packs of jackals, all feeding on the remains, with the vultures so numerous that they sometimes eat alive the newly dropped young before they can walk. Members of the herd pass within a few yards of feeding lions, sometimes stopping to stare unconcernedly at the bloody feast, instinctively knowing that they are safe till hunger again twists the cat's gut.

The extinct volcano Ngorongoro pushes up through the Rift Valley's floor, rising to seven thousand five hundred feet. From its rim, the imploded crater sweeps down two thousand feet to a natural game park of over a hundred square miles. A small forest graces one edge of the floor, bordering a landlocked saline lake. The rest of the floor seems to be empty, sunburnt grassland, with all details and animal life obliterated by the distance. Nimbus clouds cast mile-wide shadows on the floor. The air is crisp and silent. It is like standing on the edge of the world.

The zigzag track from the crater lip down to the floor, laboriously hacked from the mountain, is a one-way road down, another such track leading back out. Although appearing flat and empty from the top, the floor is rolling grassland, crisscrossed with small swamps and streams, and in places heavily laden with wait-a-bit thorn and other shrubs. Game herds are sprinkled everywhere: zebras, impalas, Thomson and Grant gazelles, but all outnumbered by the wildebeest, of which there are over ten thousand at certain times of the year. Ngorongoro Lodge on the rim guarantees "money back" if eight thousand animals are not seen during one of their game-watching trips, and that money is irretrievably theirs within half an hour after reaching the crater's floor.

Eland, hartebeest, bushbuck, reedbuck are numerous. At the forest edge elephants suck up dust and blow it over their backs; in the lake pink nostrils again betray several hippo cows, their calves and a bull. Greater flamingos with their white bodies and scarlet under-wings, wading by the hundreds in the shallows, rise in a white and pink cloud of sudden fright, intermingled with pelicans, ducks, gaudy crested cranes and a myriad of others.

With head poking through the roof opening of the landrover, one can soon sight bigger quarry in the distance, a rhino and her calf. Crossing their path, the calf hugs his mother's flank, as she charges, fearful of absolutely

nothing in this world. One teases her by slowing down several times. She prolongs her charge for near a hundred yards, only ten tantalizing feet behind the vehicle, before she gives up in disgust, stopping short, planting herself firmly on stocky legs, sides heaving, near-sighted eyes glaring contempt past her long, polished horns. Again and again she is lured into a charge, till at last the calf leads the attack, increasingly disdainful of the large but cowardly animal that the landrover proves to be.

Moving off, the landrover passes a dead zebra, with neck ripped and head kicked in, mute testimony of the gravity of African mating rivalry.

Three lions are spotted, shoulder deep in a black marsh. They do not move off, and it is difficult to understand why cats are standing in water. Then one lion lowers its head and rips open what appears to be a clod of mud—and bright red flesh shows. The cats have just hauled down a wildebeest, and hunger pushes them into the mud. One female feeds lustily, another attempts to get a morsel and receives a mud-splattering cuff across the muzzle for her trouble. The male waits too, till the female has taken the edge off her hunger, then he and the small female move in, and mud-covered chunks of flesh and gut disappear behind the ripping fangs. Panting jackals sit on the far bank of the swamp, waiting patiently. Vultures circle overhead, and a marabou stork ventures ever nearer the pride.

A mile away, four more lions growl, fling grumpy looks at the interlopers, then slink into the grass. Three cheetahs ripple through the grass in yellow blurs of flight. A hyena sits placidly in a creek.

Returning, one passes the dead zebra with the crushed skull; he has now disappeared under a maggot pile of screaming, fighting, scrabbling vultures—at least a hundred flock there. They have succeeded in turning the zebra on its back and are frenziedly ripping out its intestines, simultaneously beaking feathers jealously out of their pressing, gorging neighbors. Two marabou storks with rail-splitting, wedge-sized beaks, bloody to the eyes, stand impassively in the feathery scramble, only now and then dipping their heads. Other vultures continue to float down, long curved necks thrusting the ugly, hooked beaks lower than their spread talons as they alight for the feast.

Then the long, tortured ascent up the Windy Gap Road, distance again flattening the floor of the crater to a sunburnt, level emptiness—and once more one has that peculiar feeling of standing on the very rim of the world.

Throughout this border area roam the Masai. Herders, hunters, warriors, they are proud to the point of insolence. Truly admirable when they live within their own tradition, they are all too easily corrupted by the worst elements of "civilization." Masai males are raised by severe standards dictated by a rigid code, passing from one stage to another by age group. Starting to work as herders when young, they gradually learn the traditions of resistance to discomfort, hunger and pain, till they emerge as men, as warriors, having killed a lion with a spear. And once a warrior, the Masai's working days are over—even his mother and other wives of his father must wait upon him, catering to his whims. He becomes a dandy—a dangerous dandy—with red ocher on his face, a thin-bladed spear growing out of his hand, a cloak from shoulder to knee, beaded spangles, slit ear lobes hanging to his shoulders under the weight of metal ear rings, and a strut only forgivable in a man who has no doubts of that fact, a man who has cut the heart out of his own personal lion with a spear.

The Masai, like other peoples in Africa who count their wealth by the number of cattle in their herds, rarely slaughter their cattle. Instead, they drive a short, hollow arrow into the neck, drain off a cup of blood, seal the arrow wound, then mix curdled milk in the blood. They remain strong and healthy on this meal year round—and thus their capital never diminishes.

A few hours drive north of Nairobi lies the dream of every child—a real tree house, two stories high, built among the branches of Cape chestnut trees. "Treetops," as it is named, stands on the tree and stilts right over a swampy waterhole and a patch of ground rich in various mineral salts, judiciously abetted by a daily sprinkling of rock salt. Escort to Treetops is provided by a white

hunter with loaded rifle, a touch that brings a chuckle till one finds oneself stopped—trying to look ever smaller—by half a ton of water buffalo on the trail, which takes an inordinate time to decide whether to charge or proceed to the saltlick.

As many as five hundred of these beasts have passed through the clearing in one day, as well as three hundred elephants and herds of a dozen other species. Guests sit ten or fifteen feet above their heads as they literally eat the ground with popping crunches, and wallow and drink in the pool. It was while spending a night here in 1952 that Princess Elizabeth learned that her father King George had died and that she was now Queen.

Another hour north lies the most luxurious club in Africa—the Mount Kenya Safari Club. Practically astride the equator, with all bedrooms facing glacier-covered Mount Kenya, the country's highest mountain, one is not quite sure of being in Africa after seeing the luxury: free-form swimming pool with cocktail grotto for watching underwater swimmers, horses, a hard tennis court, trout fishing, step-down pool-size bath tubs, cypress wood fires, a putting green—and that touch which can only be Africa —a golf course with the usual rule that removing a ball from a rhino track bears no penalty. The grounds are landscaped with numerous small ponds and waterfalls covered with dozens of species of African birds, so tame they can be approached to several feet, as well as a belled duiker who roams the close-clipped lawns, pushing his tiny moist muzzle into one's hand cajoling caresses. The club was started by Hollywood's William Holden and Palm Beach millionaire Ray Ryan, "one night after too many martinis," as Ryan says. Charter members include Prince Bernhard of the Netherlands, Sir Winston Churchill, the Duke of Winchester, Conrad Hilton, Clark Gable, Lily Pons and others; travelers are admitted on temporary memberships.

Even farther north, divided by the border with Ethiopia, lies land-locked Lake Rudolph, one of the Great Rift Valley lakes, the only catchment of Ethiopia's rains other than the Nile, teeming with many kinds of fish, some reaching three hundred pounds. On its banks live the dwindling

El Molo tribe, all of whose surviving members fitted easily into one photo taken a few years ago. They are disappearing because of illness brought on by long inbreeding, and the tribe has been urged to desert their caves for farms in a fertile area. After due deliberation, the tribe decided that there were far more fish in Lake Rudolph than there were cows in the pastures, and that they would stay put, recognizing enough justice in the Government's position, however, to procure a Turkana woman to instill new blood into the tribe.

The coast of Kenya, on the Indian Ocean, is almost another world, discovered, explored and settled by a medley of peoples. The Arabs founded trading cities centuries before Christ, and in 1498, a few years after the discovery of America, Vasco da Gama visited Mombasa and Malindi on the coast. More than seventy-five years before, Malindi had sent giraffes as gifts to the Emperor of China and the Chinese had sailed to this coast, on one voyage bringing fifty-two ships with more than thirty-seven thousand men on board. Even the *Periplus of the Erythraean Sea* of the first century mentions Mombasa.

The monsoons, blowing from the northeast from November to March and from the southeast from May to September, pushed the Arab dhows back and forth across the Indian Ocean, one way carrying silks, spices and pottery, returning with cargos of slaves, ivory and aphrodisiacal rhino horn. It was for a share of this trade that the Portuguese pushed around the Cape and established watering and refueling ports on the coast, taking over Mombasa, Malindi and other towns.

Within a few years of da Gama's arrival, they had defeated Arab garrisons and taken over the entire coast north as far as Malindi, storming Mombasa in a rooftop, house-to-house battle that killed one thousand five hundred defenders and ruined the city. Nearly a hundred years later the Turks, who had replaced the Arabs as the power in Islam, conquered the coastal towns and set up headquarters in Mombasa. A Portuguese war fleet, sent from Goa, India, to recapture the town, arrived as a cannibal tribe—the Zimba, who had just captured the trade town of Kilwa and devoured three thousand defeated defenders, Arabs and Turks—was trying to force the shallow waters of Makupa ford to Mombasa Island. The Turks were defending the ford with ships, but the Portuguese fleet sunk them, and the Zimba sacked the island, celebrating with a week-long orgy of feasting on human meat.

When the Zimba marched on Malindi, the Portuguese banded with the friendly Malindi Arabs and a coastal African tribe to defeat them, and the Zimba left the coast for the interior, never to return. Taking over Mombasa, the Portuguese built Fort Jesus there, protected on one side by the sea and on the other sides by moats, as well as massive walls and hundreds of cannon.

Fort Jesus guarded the coast another hundred years for Portugal, but in 1696 Omani Arabs besieged it for almost three years. When the Fort's captain, Leonardo Barbosa, fell ill in the third year, he had his slave lowered over the wall to search for herbs. Captured by the Omani sentries, the slave revealed that death through various diseases and lack of food had reduced the defenders to Captain Barbosa, the slave, eight Portuguese soldiers, three Indians and two African women. Immediately the Arabs stormed the wall. Barbosa and others were killed, but two soldiers were captured alive. The Arabs demanded to be shown the treasury: the soldiers led them to the gunpowder magazine and set fire to a barrel of gunpowder, exploding half of the fort and taking many of their Arab conquerors with them.

Fort Jesus still stands, and all the mystery of the Orient is to be found in the Arab and Indian quarters of the Island, with their tortuous streets and teeming waterfront. The Arab dhows still ply the monsoon trade across the Indian Ocean, and the outriggers used for fishing are hand-hewed, rough-timbered, matik-sailed vessels identical to those that carried Indonesians to this coast in the fifteenth century. From Mombasa to Malindi, miles of hard-packed beach receive the bows of these ancient ships, while today's bikini beauties loll nearby, set off by the golden mica crystals that illuminate the sea and sand.

UGANDA

Between Kenya, Tanganyika and Uganda lies the lodestone of African exploration, the holy grail of geographers, the elusive mystery that tantalized kings and sages for millennia, to be discovered only a little over a hundred years ago: Lake Victoria, principal source of the river Nile.

An inland sea of twenty-seven thousand square miles, second in size only to Lake Superior, and far more famous, Victoria speeds her waters more than three thousand eight hundred miles to the sea, joining with the Blue Nile at Khartoum.

Many men struggled to discover the source of the Nile by boating or walking up the river from its mouth, Herodotus trying this in 460 B.C. But all of them were turned back by the Nile cataracts or the Sudd, the Sudan swamp across the Nile, which in rainy season reaches the size of England. There is even a legend that a Greek trader, one Diogenes, visited the area of Lake Victoria and the Mountains of the Moon by traveling overland from the Indian Ocean, shortly after the death of Christ. This information reached Ptolemy, the second-century geographer of Alexandria, and he prepared maps of surprising accuracy for the time, indicating that the Nile flowed from a pair of lakes near the equator that drained water from his *Lunae Montes.*

Whether Greek eyes saw these sights is a matter for speculation, but the route used in the attempt finally successful in solving this enigma was indeed the legendary overland route from the Indian Ocean, up five hundred miles of slave trader trails. The discoverer was John Hanning Speke, actually only second in charge to Richard Burton in the expedition that left the Indian Ocean in 1857. This was their second voyage together, both having been badly wounded and Speke momentarily captured in a dangerous journey to the forbidden Ethiopian city of Harrar, which they made disguised as natives.

After a voyage studded with difficulties, they reached Ujji, the slave post on Lake Tanganyika, which Burton believed to be the source of the Nile. While Burton stayed with Arab friends, Speke walked north for three weeks, and on August 3, 1858, saw a lake he "no longer felt any doubt . . . gave birth to that interesting river . . . ," and named it Lake Victoria. Burton maintained that the mere view of a lake was insufficient evidence for assuming that the source had been found, and they quarreled violently.

They struggled back to the coast, arriving twenty-one months after the expedition left the ocean, both ill, and Speke being carried. While Burton dawdled, Speke hastened to England, announced the discovery and was instantly lionized. Another expedition was organized with Speke in charge, but Burton—a forgotten figure, offstage, accusing Speke of perpetrating fraud—was replaced by another army officer, James Grant, who was later to participate in the British invasion of Ethiopia.

A year after leaving the Indian Ocean, Lake Victoria had still not been sighted; the column was plagued with illness, desertions, tolls for traversing territory of local chiefs, and even tribal wars. But at last on July 28, 1862, Speke, again alone—Grant having gone off to negotiate with a tribe—reached the falls where the Nile sweeps out of Victoria, naming it Rippon after the President of the Royal Geographical Society, which had sponsored the expedition.

Speke was elated: "It was a sight that attracted one for hours." But the difficult and dangerous voyage down the Nile lay ahead. It took a year to work their way down the Nile to the edge of civilization at Gondokoro, nearly two and a half years after starting the expedition. Only twenty-two out of the peak safari strength of one hundred and fifty-two reached Cairo.

But even this convincing demonstration did not put the public controversy over the Nile's source to rest. Burton continued sniping, and others—including Dr. Livingstone, who believed the Nile started farther south—pointed out that Speke had not followed the shore of the lake, and suggested that he had found only one of the minor Nile sources. A debate set between Burton and Speke to settle the issue never took place: Burton and the audience had assembled for it, only to be told that Speke had died the day before from a gunshot wound suffered while hunting.

A plaque, belated and unconvinced still, was eventually placed at Rippon Falls, giving Speke credit for finding "this"—not "the"—source of the Nile.

Final disposition of the dispute had to wait until Stanley of the *New York Herald*, finder of Livingstone, circumnavigated Lake Victoria in 1875, and Lake Tanganyika the next year, proving conclusively that Speke had indeed discovered the one true source, "the secret that even Julius Caesar yearned to unravel, but in vain."

These Victorian explorers walked across an unknown wilderness to solve the mystery of the Nile. More, they shattered forever the cocoon of centuries that had surrounded what Alan Moorehead has called a "strange little island of native civilization" that had developed in its own inconsistent manner, a civilization advanced in certain ways by millennia over some other parts of Africa shackled to the Stone Age by the paralysis of tradition.

The three kingdoms of Uganda had been relatively untouched by the outside, even by Arab traders and slavers, and had developed a unique society, most stable and advanced, in some ways similar to the great West African kingdoms.

Kings were hereditary and held absolute power, although advised by village notables. Society was organized on a hierarchical basis, and agriculture was advanced, furnishing a varied and almost European menu. Homes were large, attractive and unusual in construction, crafts were advanced—with woven straw baskets, for instance, being tight enough to hold water. Politically a shrewdly guarded balance between the three kingdoms kept war to the bare minimum of tribal skirmishing necessary to secure women and cattle.

However, some unbelievable customs and cruelties were practiced. When a king was anointed, male relatives were usually killed, unlike the Ethiopian custom of merely imprisoning them. Mutesa I, the king when Speke arrived, reputedly killed sixty of his brothers by burning them alive. Executions were nearly a daily affair at his court, sometimes several in one day, frequently for minor crimes or infractions of rules. A mere gesture from Mutesa handed down the sentence, which was carried out immediately while pounding drums drowned the screams of victims.

When Speke first met Mutesa, he presented gifts including several firearms. After Speke, at Mutesa's urging, demonstrated a pistol by shooting down a cow standing nearby, Mutesa loaded and cocked a rifle, gave it to a page, and told him to "go out and shoot a man in the outer court." Speke reports with shock that Mutesa questioned the boy to see if he had carried out the order well, but that no one showed the slightest curiosity as to the identity of the man so casually slaughtered.

Mutesa had several hundred wives in his harem at this time, and regularly received gifts of virgins from social-climbing fathers or as tribute of some kind. They came naked and greased, holding a small square of bark cloth in front of them. Some of these he gave to Speke, who passed them out as wives to his bearers. Another woman in Mutesa's court, the Queen Mother, was evidently a character in her own right. Speke writes that he inadvertently became involved in a bacchanal that ended with the Queen Mother and her attendants on hands and knees guzzling native beer from a trough.

Rumanika, king of one of the other Uganda kingdoms, had an even more intriguing harem. The women were kept so fat that they could not stand, but had to crawl around the floor. Speke measured one carefully and reports all measurements—including a fifty-two-inch bust—but said that her height of five feet eight inches was only approximate, since he could not stretch her out properly on the floor. These mountains of fat were kept in this eccentrically desirable shape by a steady and exclusive diet of milk, sucked through a straw from a pot. If the women objected to the constant imbibition—either the young who were starting, or the older who were made to keep constantly at the task—they suffered a sound thrashing with a stick or whip by the King or an attendant. Speke reports that one sixteen-year-old daughter was lovely of feature, but that "her body was round as a ball." At least, in this form, no danger existed of their being kidnapped or of their deserting the harem.

All these women, as well as the men, smoked tobacco. Most American school children, learning early that Sir Walter Raleigh discovered tobacco in Virginia and introduced it to England, causing gentlemen to be doused with water when smoke poured out of their nostrils, believe America is the only home of tobacco, but early explorers found that all Uganda tribes cultivated and smoked this native plant.

The question of seats or chairs in African societies has always been important, honor and rank being shown by the possession of a chair. Speke, after showing his displeasure at being kept waiting for a reception by Mutesa, was told he would be received at once, and that he could bring his own chair, an astounding apology and a markable courtesy. Mutesa, who imitated the gait of a lion while walking, had a most unusual chair, a page who followed him around and dropped to all fours when Mutesa wished to be seated. Like Queen Victoria, Mutesa never looked behind him; his "chair" would be there.

Mutesa, from a long line of hereditary kings, known as Kabaka, was the first to be buried in the European manner. Until his day, dead kings were embalmed, the lower jaw extracted and decorated with cowrie shells and beads. This was displayed in the tomb, while the body was buried in one of the royal burial grounds.

Mutesa still lies in the tombs on the outskirts of Kampala, along with two other Kabaka. Following tradition, women of his kingdom still care for the tombs, and various items of Mutesa are displayed there, such as his medals, utensils and weapons. Among the weapons is the gun Speke gave him, which Mutesa, fond of naming his belongings, called "They will find it when I am gone." Also there is "Bakumba-na-Mulamu," "Friend Only During Life," which is a section of Mutesa's umbilical cord preserved and honored since birth in a decorated container.

A direct descendant from Mutesa I is Edward Mutesa Kabaka today. But much has changed in Uganda. The Kabaka is also President of an independent Uganda, an educated and modern man, and the customs that shocked Speke are no more.

Even the source of the Nile that Speke and Stanley

saw has been changed. Rippon Falls, the object of centuries of speculation, search and controversy, is no more. Man has destroyed it, dynamiting the rocks and flooding the remains under ten feet of water. In 1907 Winston Churchill predicted a dam across the Nile outflow—he followed the Nile for five hundred miles by boat and bicycle—and in 1954 Queen Elizabeth dedicated that dam, a few miles downstream at Owen Falls.

Saved from submersion almost as an afterthought—an indication of the undeserved disrepute into which Speke fell—the plaque honoring him is now mounted on a red stone overlooking the watery grave of Rippon Falls, and is not easy to find, even for the handful of persons interested enough to try. Victorian punishment is as lasting as its achievements were astounding.

Near Kampala damming of the Nile has produced another change. Excessive rains since 1961 have raised Lake Victoria seven to ten feet so that lakeside villages and docks have been submerged. The excess water would drain off during the dry season if there were no Owen Falls dam, but even with all six sluice gates wide open insufficient water escapes, and the problem remains unsolved and is periodically acute.

The rise in waters has added thousands of square miles to Lake Victoria. Even so, the feat of Stanley in circumnavigating the Lake in canoes, which took fifty-seven days, can be done today from Kampala in less than a week, aboard liners providing all modern conveniences for comfortable exploration of this mysterious water, incredibly colored and mirror-flat at calm sunset, satanic black and be-surfed in a storm.

Kampala itself is a lush, tropical city built on hills, dotted with new government buildings and a whole spectrum of religious architecture, ranging from the trim Arab mosque Kubuli, built in great part by the Aga Khan's Ismailia Khoja Muslims, and the gingerbread Hindu temples, to the cathedrals of the Protestants and the Roman Catholics. A single stone cross in a small meadow six miles from town is the monument to the first African Roman Catholic saints. Twenty-five converts, including several twelve-year-old children, were martyred there—

their arms and legs were cut off and they were burned alive.

Two hundred miles down the Nile from Lake Victoria lie Murchison Falls, never seen by Speke on his march down to Egypt because he abandoned his canoes and walked overland before reaching the Falls. Although not as grand as Tisisat, it is the most powerful sight on the White Nile.

Here the Victoria Nile sweeps majestically seven hundred yards wide into the labyrinth of volcanic hills that progressively throttle it until it careens uncontrollably around the last curve and lunges down the fall through a cleft twenty feet wide, in a turbulent, frenzied race. Standing in the spray, only inches from this fury, one is deafened and dizzied.

The journey to the foot of the Falls is much less impressive, since the boats can only approach to within a half mile. But the trip on the Victoria Nile itself is an exhilarating experience. Five minutes from the dock of Paraa Lodge, past islands of the ubiquitous Nile cabbage, the launch eases into a herd of fifty hippos, snorting, groaning, sounding, then spraying water in the air like a school of whales, baring ugly six-inch tusks, trying to frighten the intruders. Only a large launch is able to venture so close—hardly a week goes by in the lakes and rivers of Uganda without a hapless African getting killed, gored or at least upset from his canoe by these river cows.

But even dead, the hippo is dangerous. Africans do not have meat often, and when a hippo is killed, either legally or by poachers, there is a sort of desperate gorging of the raw meat, people even climbing inside the corpse to feast on intestines. Knives, spears and even axes are used to chop the beast to manageable portions, and on one occasion eleven different Africans were wounded as they clawed at a dead hippo from inside while others hacked at it from without.

There are eight thousand hippos in Murchison Park alone, and even more, twelve thousand, in Queen Elizabeth National Park. Since hippos eat a hundred pounds of grass each night, they have destroyed the grazing several hundred yards back from many rivers and pools, making it necessary to forage as far as one mile.

Some of the smaller pools are like giant versions of a can of sardines: hippos leaning on each other, barrel side sliding against side as they move about, even clambering over each other in waves of effort. Such proximity frays already irascible tempers, and pairs of the largest jaws in the animal kingdom lock yawning against each other, jockeying for position to tear out a shoulder chunk, leaving the pink patch visible for weeks under the hippo's habitual covering of mud and his own dung, thrown up by his windshield-wiper-like tail. Selective shooting by Park officials is somewhat alleviating the overpopulation, but there are probably more hippos now than in the time of Speke.

The crocodiles too. They lie in masses on the sandbanks or in the shallows, rosy jaws open wide showing rows of cruel teeth, waiting for birds to land to pluck leeches from their tongueless mouths, letting the boat drift to within ten feet of them, then scurrying desperately and awkwardly on bowed legs to slide into the muddy water, where they instantly become graceful, if deadly, masters of their aquatic domain. Before reaching the hippo pool below Murchison Falls, one sees a thousand hippo and nearly as many crocodiles.

Herds of buffalo dot the banks, many of them shoulder-deep in soupy mud wallows, glaring belligerently at all intruders. The buffalo is considered the most dangerous animal in Africa. He is vengeful, and will stalk man, not fleeing when wounded like other animals, but circling silently and unseen till the short, crushing rush. Even when the victim escapes by climbing a tree, the buffalo persists. If the tree is small and a boot dangles within reach, he will attack in his own fashion. The buffalo's tongue is tough, rougher than sharkskin, and he licks at the boot. He rasps till the boot is worn away, and then he licks at the flesh. Bodies have been found, self-lashed in trees before death, life blood drained to the ground along dangling leg bones, fleshless to the knees.

Small herds of elephants water along the way, flapping ears, shaking trunks and tusks, frustrated in their attempts to charge or frighten the boat, finally turning and lumbering into the bush enraged. Frustrating the elephant is not so easy on land. Upon entering the Park, a sign warns that "Elephants have right of way," a sensible warning since there are nine thousand elephants in Murchison's eleven thousand square miles, and a car rarely travels a track without being delayed, sometimes as much as several hours, by herds of elephants browsing back and forth across the way. Patience is a real virtue, it being too frequent—including one case in 1964 of two women tourists —to find missing cars and occupants flattened into the ground by the stomping—that peculiar blood-lust stomping, of aroused elephants.

At the park lodge itself, elephants are common, incongruously scratching themselves against a straining sheet metal shed, passing the restaurant at mealtimes, or even mothers trailed by babies backing guests into their lodges, threatening to charge, only turning away when the guest disappears behind closed doors—doors quite ineffectual to stop a charge.

In the west of Uganda bordering the Congo—not blocking the Nile's rush to the sea from Lake Victoria, as Burton claimed—rear the Ruwenzori Mountains, the famous Mountains of the Moon, thirty miles of glaciers, with the twin peaks of Margherita and Alexandra, nearly seventeen thousand feet high. Year round these mountains are hooded by clouds, and it is a rare traveler who has seen more than the tumbled dark slopes disappearing into the swirling mists. In certain seasons, toward sunset, these clouds seem to explode in sullen rage, racing down across the crater lakes in Queen Elizabeth Park and out across Lake Edward. The air stills, expectant, oppressive, then the first fingers of cloud stretch out from the banks on the peaks, dragging behind them larger masses of billowing vapor, quickly overtaking the fingers and forming a black front that seems to roll over and down itself in a rush, following the downward pitch of the land to the lake, blackening the blue sky, staining the land and water with the same black as the storm races to catch the sun. Chasing the furious front come the blind sheets of water, curtains from cloud to earth, whose trailing ends puncture the wind-driven clouds, slap and buffet the thirsty red earth into a submissive quagmire.

RHODESIAS

Just as the Nile cuts through half of Africa, so it has flowed through the history of the continent.

It was the lure of the Nile that ensnared that legendary giant of African exploration, Dr. David Livingstone, sending him through the Rhodesias, and finally bringing him to his death in Zambia in a last painful quest for the river's source—ten years after Speke had already found it.

This indomitable Scotsman inked in more lines on the blank spaces of the African map than any other explorer. He started his African career as a teaching missionary among the Tswana tribes of South Africa—even writing after the fever of exploration had gripped him: "I would not be content to be an explorer only, but a missionary first and a geographer by the way."

Ten years in the missionary schools passed before Livingstone left his family behind and first walked north; from then on he was explorer. He crossed two hundred and fifty miles of the great Kalahari Desert of Bechuanaland to Lake Ngami, and onward to discover the Zambezi rising in the hills of Angola and flowing across the continent to pour into the Indian Ocean.

Livingstone felt the Zambezi might be "a highway capable of being traversed by boats to an entirely unexplored and very populous region," a highway that could open up the more profitable commercial trade that would stifle the slave trade that he hated so much.

He turned west at the Zambezi—seemingly following the immutable instinct of explorers seeking the sources of African rivers. For two years he plodded two thousand miles through virgin savannah highlands and jungle to the Atlantic Ocean. For this monumental journey he carried three muskets, a rifle, a shotgun, twenty pounds of beads, clothes, medicine, a Bible, sextant, a compass, a thermometer, a tent and some blankets—absurdly inadequate equipment for traversing an unknown continent.

The vast expanse of water shocked his bearers. "Then it is not true what the ancients taught us, that the world has no end! All at once it says to us, 'I am finished. There is no more of me.'" Some of these bearers were given to him by a Chief Sekeletu, who had traveled a hundred miles to see and talk with this first white man on the Zambezi, and were to stay with Livingstone through most of his expeditions.

He refused passage to England, and turning back into the jungle, determined to follow the Zambezi to its mouth. They were paddling down the river in 1855 when he first saw "five columns of vapour rising two hundred and fifty feet to mingle with the clouds"—Mosi-Oa-Tunya, the Smoke that Thunders. His paddlers beached the pirogues on a small island—now Livingstone Island—at the lip of the Falls. "Scenes so lovely must have been gazed upon by Angels in their flight," he wrote, and the description does not seem extravagant. He named the Falls after Queen Victoria.

Dotted with islands, placid, almost oil slick, the Zambezi flows lazily to the eighteen-hundred-yard brink of the Falls, then lunges over five separate waterfalls three hundred and fifty feet to the shattered rock below. The Falls are one and a half times as wide and twice as high as those of Niagara. Breaking against the rock below—there is no fall pool as such—the water climbs back up the turbulent air as clouds of spray, sometimes to five thousand feet, visible twenty-five miles away, and fanning into a permanent veil laced always with at least one shimmering rainbow. When the full moon shines, a lunar rainbow, a moonbow, arcs the Falls.

In the dry season, two million gallons of water plunge over the brink in one minute, and during the April flood, seventy-five million gallons, pushing up a spray that obscures the Falls completely for days on end. During the continual cloudbursts of 1958, the flow engulfing the Falls rose to one hundred and fifty million gallons a minute. The spray nourishes a rain forest in front of the Falls.

On the river bank, overlooking this cataclysm, broods a huge bronze statue of Livingstone. Lifelike, his walking stick, Bible and field glasses in hand, flapped cap in place, he stares endlessly at the Mosi-Oa-Tunya, apparently as transfixed as the visitor at sight of this natural wonder.

After portaging the Falls, Livingstone continued

downstream. It was on this journey that he was attacked by a lion that crushed his shoulder, a wound that was to give him difficulty till his death. Farther on, he saw the African gold miners bury swatches of cloth, believing them to be gold seed, seed of golden fruit that they could harvest later.

Following the river to the sea, Livingstone arrived half dead from malaria and dysentery, more than four years after starting on this voyage. He returned to England to a hero's welcome. Victorian England devoured books on exploration and geography with the avid interest today reserved for news of television and movie stars. An authentic explorer in person was showered with adulation.

A new expedition under Livingstone and financed by the Government was quickly dispatched. It was lavishly equipped even with a steamship to explore the navigational possibilities of the Zambezi. But Livingstone's "highway of commerce" was frustrated by the rapids of Kebrabasa, and the ship proved useful only in discovering Lake Nyasa.

Disappointed with the results, the Government recalled Livingstone and withdrew its financial support. Undaunted, even though losing his wife on the last expedition, within a year Livingstone had organized another, financed by friends and book sales. The Government did name him British consul, without salary, "for that portion lying between Portuguese Africa and Abyssinia." But there were no steamboats, and a minimum of other equipment.

This voyage was Livingstone's longest, lasting from 1865 to 1873. It was in difficulty from the start, and he himself was never to return. Livingstone's pack animals soon died, and many of his men deserted, leaving him with only nine porters. Worse, his medicine kit was stolen a few months after he started. Prophetically, Livingstone wrote, "I felt as though I had received sentence of death." Even after this disaster, it was not too late to turn back to the coast, but like a man possessed, he trekked on.

In central Zambia he spent many months at the kraal of Chief Kazembe, a despotic ruler whose kraal gate was hung with severed human ears, limbs and heads. Kazembe conducted a lucrative trade with the Arabs from the Indian

Ocean ports, and blocked all westward travelers for fear his monopoly might be broken. Livingstone met people in the kraal who recalled one man who had tried.

Dr. Francisco de Lacerda, a doctor of mathematics and Royal Astronomer, attempted to march from the Indian Ocean to the Atlantic in 1798. Moving out with sixty-two Portuguese soldiers and four hundred slaves as porters, Lacerda struggled as far as Kazembe's village. Upon arrival he was so sick he was being carried, and many of the slaves had escaped. Eight weeks passed while Kazembe refused to see them. Finally he granted an audience on the day Lacerda died of fever. Father Pinto, second in command, waited another fruitless eight months for permission to travel west, till his troops mutinied and left with the rest of the slaves for the Indian Ocean. Pinto, struggling back with a few faithful, was refused supplies and aid by tribes the mutineers had turned against him, in the hope their treachery would die with him. But he made it, and they were punished.

At Kazembe's kraal Livingstone found traces also of the only other people who had ever matched his crossing from ocean to ocean—the Portuguese half-breeds Pedro João Baptista and Amaro Jose, from Angola. These uneducated predecessors of today's *assimilados*, one being literate enough to keep a rudimentary diary, left Luanda on the Atlantic in 1802 and walked into the Indian Ocean port of Tete ten years later—four of those years being spent as honored guests and prisoners at the kraal of Chief Kazembe. Not content with this extraordinary achievement, they walked back to the Atlantic Ocean.

It was at Kazembe's kraal that Livingstone witnessed —as did Lacerda before him—the all-encompassing power of the charge of witchcraft, or evil-eye. Persons accused would go to any lengths, travel any distance, to clear themselves, voluntarily appearing for the auto-da-fé. They quaffed a tincture of bark potion—innocent if unscathed, guilty if harmed. Since the sap of the tree chosen for the potion was poisonous, the "witch" invariably suffered a slow and agonizing death.

Short of supplies, buffeted by local wars, Livingstone

became increasingly dependent on the Arab slave traders, whose ravages sickened him. In one village market he watched helplessly as slave traders, evidently incensed at the price asked for a chicken, fired into the crowd, driving many of them including women and children into the river, senselessly slaughtering over three hundred. Livingstone's description of this atrocity—finally carried to the world by Stanley because the Arabs refused to forward his mail—more than any other single circumstance aroused English ire over slavery. Just a few months after Livingstone's death, the Sultan of Zanzibar was forced to close the centuries-old slave market.

Revolted by this butchery, Livingstone left the Arab caravan and returned to the slaving headquarters at Ujiji on Lake Tanganyika, where he had left some stores and hoped to find medicine brought up by one of the regular caravans from Zanzibar. The medicine had not arrived, his stores were plundered and there was not even any mail. Livingstone fell into despair.

In this pitiful state, on November 10, 1871, Livingstone saw a white man appear out of the bush, and heard the words most often associated with African tales of exploration: "Dr. Livingstone, I presume?"

Henry Morton Stanley had found Livingstone for the *New York Herald* and an anxious world. Only thirty years old at the time, Stanley—a Welshman naturalized American—went on to solve the riddle of the Nile, explore the Congo basin and build himself a reputation as one of the great explorers of Africa. Honors were heaped upon him; he eventually became a member of the British Parliament, and was knighted. Livingstone himself, apart from his funeral, was never so honored by England.

Stanley was able to spare some food and medicine, and Livingstone's condition improved greatly. For some weeks they explored the edges of Lake Tanganyika together, but Livingstone adamantly refused to return to civilization. The Nile called still. In his travels he had seen a great river, the Lualaba, flowing to the north. He determined to find its source—reported to be somewhere south of Lake Bangweulu in Zambia—and follow it to its

mouth. Confident the Lualaba would prove to be the Nile
—in reality it is the headwater of the Congo River—
Livingstone felt this achievement in one swoop would
complete and justify his life's explorations.

But his flickering health failed. Ill, and unable to
continue in the torrential rains, he was carried into the
kraal of Chitambo, a few miles south of Lake Bangweulu,
in the last days of April, 1873. His longest exploration
was almost at an end. He had written a few weeks before:
"Oh! how I long to be permitted by the Over Power to
finish my work." But the indomitable will was not matched
by the body. On May 1 in the early hours, he was found
slumped over his bed; he had died while praying.

The influence and power of this man over those who
met him, and the many who knew him only through his
writings, was best illustrated by the subsequent actions
of his servants, Susi and Chuma. At Chitambo's kraal,
they cut his heart out and buried it under a tree, a tree
marked today by a small monument. They sprinkled his
body with salt, and dried it in the sun for two weeks. Then
they sewed it in cloth, bark and a tarp, lashed it to a pole,
and carried it for a year the thousand miles to Zanzibar.

The body was identified by the lion-clawed shoulder,
and it was transported to England for burial in Westminster Abbey. England and the world mourned him.

Only five months after Livingstone died, a young
man walked into the diamond fields just discovered in
Griqualand, where Livingstone had been a missionary.
He was destined to mark this land more tangibly than
Livingstone. Fifth son of an English preacher, penniless,
driven to emigrate to South Africa because of a bad lung
condition, within two years he was rich. He eventually
became one of the most powerful men in South Africa,
and was responsible for bringing the territories of Northern and Southern Rhodesia and Bechuanaland under
the British flag.

Cecil John Rhodes was the complete antithesis of
Livingstone. He was a convinced colonialist, an unabashed
empire builder, a man who used his persuasive abilities
to push native chiefs into concessions that eventually

robbed them of their kingdoms. An imperialist when the word was a distinct compliment, he dreamed of an Imperial Way under the British flag from the Cape to Cairo—"I want to see all that red, British red; this is my dream!" He believed the English were the most capable people in the world, and that the more land they occupied, the better it was for the world.

Rhodes persuaded Lobengula, the Ndebele king who controlled great parts of Rhodesia, to grant him a concession to all metals and minerals in his kingdom. This Lobengula did, signing with the king's mark over the royal elephant seal. With this, and a similar concession signed by Lewanika, who controlled parts of Zambia, Rhodes obtained a charter from the British Government to settle the area. "Our concession is so gigantic, it is like giving a man the whole of Australia," Rhodes wrote jubilantly.

Armed caravans of settlers moved in immediately; posts and towns were set up; permanent buildings were constructed; a mail service started; and even grass was sown. The first caravan of six hundred men was temporarily surrounded by Lobengula's impi of eighteen thousand men—which could easily have crushed the whites—but Lobengula wanted to negotiate peacefully with the white man and managed to dissuade his angry chiefs. He tried every method short of force to stop the settlements. He even returned the gold and rifles and ammunition he was paid for the concession, but all in vain. He compared his situation to that of a fly stalked by a chameleon, "that advances slowly and gently, first putting forward one leg, then another, until at last he darts out his tongue."

With this restless and powerful native army as a sword of Damocles, Rhodes became convinced a military defeat of the Ndebele was necessary for further settlement. Lobengula's last peace mission was arrested on false charges, while Rhodes cut himself off from communication by a sea voyage till his armed columns set off to attack.

In two separate battles Rhodes' machine guns decimated an Ndebele impi of about five thousand men. Many of the surviving warriors, never before having known

defeat, committed suicide rather than return to their
~~~~~ in disgrace. Lobengula set fire to the royal kraal,
                              s and fled toward the
                          d men following Loben-
                          and foolishly attempted
                          d, but Lobengula himself
                          ezi. There were other
                          e colonization swept on
                          is fly. Lobengula's plain-
                          dors of history: "I only

                          Rhodesia, buying a two-
                          le is buried in the high-
                          te hill he called his "view
                          eral cortege, the Ndebele
                          ty miles, silently paying
                          d betrayed their trust.
                          When Rhodes pushed his
                          d the Indian Ocean port
                          were frequently delayed
                          tusked up the track as
                          ces of an erector set. The
                          sy fodder of the settlers'
                          he game. Africans, hungry
                          ns. Colonial soldiery shot
                          the ivory, to pay for their
                          took great pride in killing
                          Karamoja Bell boasted of
                          bull elephants a day, and
                          sixty rhinos within sixty
days. The rhino has always been a special target, since its
horns—not really horn, but a tightly packed growth of
hair or keratinous material—are considered by Orientals
to be a particularly effective aphrodisiac when ground
into powder. Even today a rhino horn is worth a small
fortune. Poachers, that modern menace to game—moti-
vated probably as much by hunger as by gainful greed—
constantly stalk rhinos all over Africa. Perhaps the rhino's
seemingly unreasonable penchant for charging anything
that moves is in fact quite reasonable.

Disease indirectly decimated the wild game further.

They are natural carriers of the parasite trypanosome, given them by the tsetse fly. Unaffected themselves, they pass it on to cattle and humans, causing the fatal sleeping sickness. For this they were slaughtered by the thousand—a dubious remedy that is resorted to even today.

In spite of the staggering loss of animals—millions upon millions—game parks today preserve great numbers of most species. The animals are not protected from each other or nature, but man's depredations are curbed to a maximum. Over eight thousand elephants survive in Zambia's Luangwa Valley game preserve, along with swarms of other game. Protected by an armed white hunter, groups wander the bush for game-watching on foot. Kafue park, outside of Lusaka, jacaranda- and flamboyant-bedecked capital of Zambia, is as big as Massachusetts or New Jersey and prowled by thousands of lion. In Livingstone game park near Victoria Falls, one of the rare fenced parks, zebras are so tame they hang their heads in car windows and snuff at pockets, begging sugar.

Upstream from the Falls, the river is dotted with islands, one of them, King George Island, ruled by a pack of vervet monkeys that swing out of the trees to beg or steal anything that looks like food from picnickers. In dry season, the elephants from drying Bechuanaland come to drink, and they wade to King George Island, hosing themselves delightedly, unabashedly delirious in the deliciousness of water in abundance. The Island furnishes a favorite food, the ivory palm, whose fruit has an ivory-like, walnut-size, seed. This palm grows only where the elephant travels, the fruits eaten and the seeds left behind to be fertilized by his foot-high cylinders of dung.

Game-viewing flights take off near Victoria Falls to rival Livingstone's Angels, winging over Bechuanaland and the Kalahari Desert, swooping to run the game herds that roam as widely as ever they did in the time of Rhodes. Curving over Mosi-Oa-Tunya, the flight reveals the bizarre geology of the Falls and gorges.

Beneath the spray the Zambezi seems to plunge straight into the ground, for the river does not continue

in a straight line. It flows over the side of a narrow gorge that from the air appears to be the top line of a Z. This line, the gorge, is a half mile in length. At the end of the gorge the river cuts back sharply, down the diagonal of the Z to its lower line: another angle, another gorge. Over the millions of years, the Zambezi has carved a zigzag of these gorges, eight in all, each over three hundred feet deep, each of whose upstream edges was once the lip of the falls, each lip abandoned as the Zambezi carved a new arm to the continuous Z. At today's lip, a fissure at one end, Devil's Cataract, has already been eaten fifty feet lower than the rest of the Falls, and will eventually— half a million years—form the ninth gorge.

Where the Zambezi drops out of the present fall gorge, a hundred yards down the diagonal, a Boiling Pot has formed, a circular pool that rises as much as fifty-six feet during flood, wheeling into a whirlpool that sometimes spins for weeks the bodies of hippos that have washed over the Falls.

Seventy miles downstream from Victoria Falls lies Kariba dam, a narrow passage in the hills in Livingstone's time, now a dam two thousand feet long and four hundred fifty feet high, backing up the longest man-made lake in the world, one hundred seventy-five miles, a title that will be usurped by the Aswan dam on the Nile in Egypt when its lake fills to its three-hundred-mile limit.

Kariba Lake, like most of the Zambezi, is rich with exotic African fish: the vundu, recorded up to three hundred and sixty-eight pounds, the squeakers, which actually bark and carry dangerous poison in their fins, the air-breathing lungfish and the hundred-pound barbell, which emits painful electric shocks.

Electricity is Kariba's forte, electricity that runs the metal industries of both Zambia and Rhodesia. In Rhodes' time the expected gold and other minerals extracted from the hole Lobengula gave him were disappointingly sparse. But at last, the promise is being fulfilled. Over forty different minerals are mined in the two countries, including lead, zinc, tin, copper, cadmium, selenium, manganese, cobalt, silver, rubies, gold, diamonds and emeralds.

In northern Zambia, along the border with Katanga —a native word meaning green rock—there are mountains of copper ore, over seven hundred million tons, with veins up to sixty feet thick—a fifth of the world's proven reserves.

It was here, in a deep cave broken into by modern high-speed mining drills cutting the shaft of Broken Hill mine, that were found the fossilized remains of Homo Rhodesiensis, an ancient African, though not as old as the Nutcracker Man of Olduvai Gorge. Farther toward the Tanganyikan border, the floor of Kalambo Gorge is littered with stone tools, wooden digging sticks, throwing clubs; even a wooden knife was found here, all discarded by the "Handax Culture" people thirty-six thousand years ago. Into this eerie abyss, this puncture in the African mesa, drops the continent's second highest waterfall in a narrow unbroken water arc of seven hundred and twenty-six feet down the sheer cliff to the sunless depths below. Meandering across the plateau, the stream plunges, then seems to disappear as it flows down the floor of the fissure, masked by the overhanging cliffs. The marabou scavenger stork breeds in this rift, and flocks of the giant birds with still, fluted wings ride the turbulent air currents, spiraling up from the fall pool into the sun above.

Zambia's copperbelt is matched in Rhodesia by the Great Dyke, a three-hundred-mile-long mountainous back-bone of mineral wealth. Ground water draining from this Dyke has hollowed out a labyrinth of caverns near there known as the Sinoia Caves, not far from Rhodesia's skyscraper-dotted capital, Salisbury.

In one of the caverns the "Sleeping Pool" fills a subterranean cradle nearly as deep as the gorge of Victoria Falls. A mere twenty yards across, the Pool has been plumbed to three hundred and fifteen feet. The surface of the Pool is one hundred and fifty feet underground, but the roof directly over the Pool fell in centuries ago. Through this rupture, the sun pours light into the still depths below, reflecting the sky in intense shades of blue that change with the angle of the sun, from a soft angora through a scintillating ceramic to a deep metallic cobalt.

The sloping cave that leads to the shore of the Pool focuses like a telescope on this aqueous jewel below.

Small gold and silver fish arc through the blue limpidity, and silt on the Pool's floor has surrendered microscopic creatures unknown anywhere else in the world. Africans believed a great serpent fed there. Their name for the Pool was Chirorodziva, Pool of the Fallen, so named when early in the nineteenth century migrating Angoni tribesmen defeated a local tribe and hurled their captives through the cave's roof to the subterranean depths below.

At the southern extremity of this Great Dyke, eight thousand miles from Jerusalem, King Solomon haunts again. Here, in a saucer of massive granite hills, spreads the ancient city of Great Zimbabwe, walls, homes and a temple, a sanctuary and fortress of disputed age and origin. Early explorers and some Africans vaunted Zimbabwe as the site of King Solomon's lost gold mines.

The first white man to see Zimbabwe was an American, Adam Renders, a hunter who discovered the ruins in 1868. He died and was buried there a few years later, but his grave is lost among the tumbled blocks of Zimbabwe. From these massive ruins, Renders and others carried off gold jewelry, figurines covered in gold leaf, phallic symbols, carved soapstone pillars and copper ornaments, as well as pottery, beads and other items of trade from distant India and China.

The heart of Zimbabwe is the Temple, a great elliptical wall thirty-two feet high and sixteen feet thick at its base, enclosing the ruins of dwellings, internal defensive dividing walls and a conical tower thirty-four feet high. Little is known of the religious practices of Zimbabwe's people, but this conical tower is believed to have been the center of fertility rites.

Lower than the Temple on the saucer's floor lies the Valley of Ruins, strewn with rock homes, the inspiration for the Dead City in Rider Haggard's novel *She*. Many of these homes were torn down by treasure hunters, searching for caches of gold.

Above the Temple and the Valley of Ruins, crowning a precipitous granite outcropping, looms the "Acropolis."

This is the fortress of Zimbabwe, the first construction in the city. Defense works are a complex of rooms and platforms, inner and outer walls built to the edge of the nearly vertical ascents, and ingeniously incorporating seventy-foot outcropping boulders.

All the construction at Zimbabwe was of hand-hewn granite blocks mounted without mortar. The wall of the temple alone is reckoned to contain fifteen thousand tons of stone. This granite was mined by building huge fires on outcrops, then dousing the heated stone with cold water till great slabs flaked off. These were laboriously hand-shaped, and carried the several miles to the construction sites by slaves—a work of centuries.

Centuries were available. First construction according to archaeologists started "before 300 A.D." and last construction was finished by 1800. But Zimbabwe was sacked in 1833 by Nguni invaders, and eventually abandoned.

The wealth to build so massively is believed to have been based on the hinterland's now defunct gold trade with the Arab ports of the Indian Ocean littoral. Gold-working rooms were found on the Acropolis, as well as many gold artifacts that survived the depredations of early treasure hunters. And abandoned gold suggests either an incredible panic or a surplus of the heavy metal.

It is this gold that has nurtured the legend that Zimbabwe was Solomon's lost mine. Opponents of the Solomon legend claim Zimbabwe was not the outpost of that Oriental potentate but the capital of a native African empire that sprawled across and beyond the borders of Rhodesia, ruled by King Monomotapa. They especially cherish two pieces of wood delved from the Temple's footing. They were radioactive carbon-dated to A.D. 591 and A.D. 702, dates long after Solomon was dead.

But Monomotapa is a vulgarization of the original African Mwana Wa Tapa, Lord of the Mines, and no one has proved how long Zimbabwe existed before the present temple was constructed. The presence of Chinese goods is proof of extensive trade, and the mining and fashioning of gold in quantity leaves open the possibility that this may indeed have been the source of Solomon's treasures.

The truth is not known yet. It never will be known, probably. Perhaps because of this, or perhaps merely because of the weird whine of African winds, whistling through the deserted labyrinth of a lost civilization under the blistering African sun, the traveler is apt to listen to his diaphanous soul: he hears the warning drum from the outpost, he sees the caravan born of the yearly monsoon. Solomon's envoy leaves the litter, the Lord of Mines awaits. The feasting and fornication find license, the treasure of trinket bead and inlay changes place with the dull yellow metal. The envoy mounts his Nubian-born litter to return a year hence to dandle his progeny on his knee. The horn sounds, and the traveler mounts his bus to read his guide book, to learn that what he saw was but a madness—common under the African sun.

Two Worlds

Conventionally, Africa has been divided into Arab and Negro worlds by the Sahara. But there is another division, a dichotomy within Black Africa of east and west.

In the east—Ethiopia, Kenya, Tanzania—the land leaves the sea and rapidly rises to a high plateau of ten thousand feet, with peaks as high as nineteen thousand. In the west, the gradient is gentle and the highest peak is but a little over five thousand feet. The eastern highlands are semi-arid, sparsely vegetated, quickly mounting above the reach of malaria, and warm clothing is necessary at night. In the west, long known as the White Man's Grave, jungle forests choke the earth far inland from the sea, malaria is prevalent over a wider range, and sleep is a wet and sticky effort. In the highlands the horizon is distant and crystalline, and the sky, somehow, seems closer to the ground than anywhere else in the world, while the west coast rarely displays a clear sky. Humidity and heat haze gray the air and block the sun, sometimes hiding it till it peers forth like a midday moon. In the east, animals outnumber man; in the west, man is more prolific.

Winds bred by the sun's heat have fostered this dichotomy further. From November to March the monsoon blows

out of the northeast, sweeping across the Indian Ocean, scooping up moisture and spilling it out of clouds over the east coast. From May to September, the process is reversed. Southeast trade winds skim across the Atlantic and deluge the west coast. These alternating winds have been used for millennia by Arabs, Indians, Chinese and even Indonesians to trade with and colonize the east coast. But there were no peoples in the south Atlantic that could use the winds to carry them to the west coast. And Europeans inching along the west coast from the north were stopped for centuries at Cape Bojador by the strong currents and winds. Only when the Portuguese adopted the lateen sail—a Mediterranean specialty that enabled them to sail closer to the wind and guarantee their return—was the Cape finally turned.

All these contrapuntal forces, especially the winds, have decisively influenced the different development of the two profiles of Black Africa, differences readily apparent to the traveler. Once the dichotomy is noted, however, it paradoxically fades from the conscious. Although separate and opposite, Black Africa's profiles are far more alike than different, bound together about the many-layered core of the African identity.

CAMEROONS

Portuguese navigators explored the coasts of Africa and turned the Cape of Good Hope. But there is evidence that other people had sailed these coasts long before, and had even established towns.

Six centuries before the birth of Christ, Phoenicians from Carthage were pushing ships through the Pillars of Hercules at Gibraltar and coasting south down the Atlantic seaboard. The greatest of these expeditions was led by Hanno of Carthage, and his personal epic exists today, taken in a Greek translation from the plaque Hanno erected in the Temple of Moloch upon his return to Carthage. Hanno wrote that he was commissioned "to sail past the Pillars of Hercules, and to found cities of the Libyphoenicians. He set sail with sixty vessels of fifty oars and a multitude of men and women to the number of thirty thousand, and provisions and other equipment." Hanno founded cities on the coast of Africa that are inhabited today, two thousand five hundred years later.

At one point, his tale of the voyage reads: "We left in a hurry and coasted along a country with a fragrant smoke of blazing timber, from which streams of fire plunged into the sea. The land was unapproachable for heat. So we sailed away in fear, and in four days' journey saw the land ablaze by night. In the center a leaping flame towered above the others and appeared to reach the stars. This was the highest mountain that we saw: it was called the Chariot of the Gods."

The highest mountain on the west coast of Africa is Mount Cameroon, thirteen thousand three hundred and seventy feet, a quiescent but active volcano. The country around shows that there has been volcanic activity not too long ago. Hanno's "Chariot of the Gods" is believed by many to have been this peak, Mount Cameroon, erupting and firing the surrounding forests. But, as in most history of exploration, there is a controversy: some claim Hanno saw nothing more than burning grass in southern Morocco.

It was two thousand years before Fernaño do Po and his Portuguese sailing vessels heaved to in the Wouri River estuary and dropped anchor. His sailors saw thousands of shrimp, or *camarões*, in the shallow waters, and so the Cameroons were named. The Douala natives there gave their name to the port, today a thriving modern city, thirty-five miles from Mount Cameroon. But rare is the day when this rugged peak cuts the sky cleanly. It is usually lost in the shimmering heat haze that hangs over this tropical coast like a shroud, turning the sun into a pale afternoon moon. On some days the haze so thickens that even the pirogue fishermen stay on the beach—fishermen capable of taking twelve-foot sharks with the most primitive methods in these tree-trunk dugouts.

The Portuguese were not colonizers as were the Phoenicians. And the Cameroons were tucked too far under the bulge of Africa to serve ships seeking the shortest run to the Cape and India. Slavers, traders and missionaries from other European countries arrived and worked the coast, but they did not penetrate the country till the late nineteenth century. They knew only the coast, this inhospitable coast.

The Atlantic slams into the land here, fighting to conquer it, make it part of the sea. Along a third of this coast, it has almost succeeded, as at high tide it surges into the mangrove swamps that stretch back from the shore. Mangrove trees—squatting obscenely on their many-jointed arms, oyster-encrusted at low tide, a legion of crouching black spiders awaiting a victim—separate reluctantly to form the slender, twisting water passages. Pirogues ply these passages for miles, slipping through the black, silent waters, hastening across the swamp from land to land. Nothing seems to live here, and nothing much of anything does. If not winning back the land, the ocean at least denies it to man.

But the Cameroons are so much more than a mangrove swamp. They are a microcosm of the entire continent of Africa. Like a long, narrow triangle, they seem to hang from the tip of Lake Tchad. Flying from Lake Tchad, swampy borders below give way to white desert, then shade to arid bush land, flat and empty, sown with thorn bush, and a cover of dessicated shrubs grudgingly keeping a few goats and sheep from starvation. Farther south, the bush melds into the dun savannah plains, green-splashed with groves of trees, grooved with rare riverbeds, dry except in the rains. Only a few wells and springs give limited year-round water.

Flitting evenly across the flat plateau, the plane's shadow suddenly bounces violently into the first of the tangle of canyons that ends the plains. Small peaks, mesas, badlands and more canyons follow—from the air deserted, and even on the parsimonious ground, meagerly populated. The wasted brown changing to grizzled green, then a lush verdure, gives the first clue that the plane has arrived over the fertile central valleys and hills. Abrupt angles of uneroded rock give way to rounded slopes of land watered well and extensively, watered by the last dregs in the monsoon winds, the leftovers from the torrents that have drenched the forests to the south and west.

From the air, this forest appears as monotonous and dead as the desert, a flat, lifeless green carpet stretching to the mangrove swamps and the sea. The calm deceives. This impenetrable jungle is really a world at war, a world of intense stillness, perpetual twilight and a deadly, silent vegetal struggle to mount to the life-giving world of light.

In the south, near Kribi, where there is no swamp, and the rain forest marches right up to the sea, the ocean has thrown up miles of white sand, studded with tall palms that grow to the tide mark, leaning in swoops out over the crashing surf. Inland from here, pygmies are masters of the rain forest jungle, hunting and wandering this vast domain where other peoples would expire.

Some stay so deep in the forest that no outsider ever sees them. Others have been more or less "domesticated" in that the Government has persuaded them to leave their traditional forest wanderings and settle down in mud and grass huts fifteen or twenty miles outside of Kribi. When one visits them, the children are liable not to be there, but rather in school learning to read and write. These pygmies even wear Western dress of sorts, although when they go to the jungle, they don scanty and practical skin and bark clothing. When first seen in front of their huts, they appear too big, of a stature no different from anyone else, much larger than pygmies should be. Regular African features, a lack of hesitantly expected dwarf characteristics, strengthen this impression.

But they are tiny. The huts are shoulder high, and the tallest among the pygmies comes only to the shoulder of a short American woman.

The old saw "Dynamite comes in small packages" seems justified here. Small as he is, the pygmy is indeed, as his African neighbors dub him, "King of the Forest." He lives by hunting, either as a formidable marksman with his stunted bow and arrows so easy to pass through the congested forests, or with hunting net. A quarter-mile-long hand-made net is spread in the forest, then men, women and children beat drums, crash through the brush, pound on the trees, and scream. Covering a large funnel-shaped part of the forest, they drive all game—duikers, warthogs, reedbucks—before them into the net. There the victims thrash with tangled legs and horns till a quick knife slits throats, and the women start skinning.

The courage of this diminutive huntsman even leads him to attack and kill elephants with his short spear. Sometimes this is done by a group of pygmies who rush an elephant in the bush, thrust spears in him, and flee his enraged agony. But more often they find an elephant's trail and dig a small, skillfully concealed slit in it; then a pygmy—thoroughly rubbed with elephant dung—slips in. He crouches there hours, or even days, till an elephant passes over, then lodges the spear deeply in the elephant's belly, cowering in the hole and entreating his animist gods that the elephant running amuck among the splintering trees will not detect pygmy odor through the elephant dung.

Once the wounded elephant tires of searching for his tormentor and sways off through the forest, the entire pygmy band, women and children included, trails slowly after him, sometimes traveling two weeks and two hundred miles before the spear cuts enough gut and the behemoth falls to his knees, toppling to block the track with his gargantuan mass, bubbling out his last shrill trumpeted protest.

Materializing magically, pygmies circle, where a moment before there were but columned ranks of trees. One approaches tentatively, jabs a spear in the powerful but tender trunk. No movement. The elephant is dead, far from his legendary graveyard. The circle closes, then bursts into delighted laughter and jabbering, as some start hacking at the armor-like skin near the bloody and rotting belly wound, the first morsel sacrificed to the god of hunt, and others give a leg up to clamber onto this small mountain to slice and gouge and feast. They spend a week at the kill, bellies further distended each day, till what is left of useful meat, ivory, bone and skin can be carried back with the hunters to their retreat. The oldest and youngest have kept the fires burning, hungry and impatient in their waiting.

The return is triumphal, a feast till dawn, music and dance exhilarating and exhausting warrior and woman. It is the same after every hunt, but the return from the big annual hunt for their great religious feast, which curiously enough coincides generally with the Christmas and New Year's week, is the most abandoned, and lasts till stamina, bouyed by gluttonous intake of meat and beer, finally collapses.

The most amazing fact about the pygmy is that he is alive, alive and flourishing after centuries in this jungle— jungle that barred human migration for millennia—able to live in this trackless maze, to travel swiftly and silently, always knowing without compass where he is and how long it will take to be at another place where he has never been, inured to the hardships, able to extract life-sustaining tubers among the many poisons, interpreting skillfully the jungle signs of danger and opportunity, unshakable on a spoor. It is said a half hoofprint can tell the pygmy the weight, size and even sex of the animal that impressed it, as well as how many minutes or days ago the track was made, and whether the animal was feeding, fleeing or playing. A snake's rippling passage he follows by smell alone.

Sharing the remoter regions of this green cathedral with the pygmy, even shyer than him, and the most

unbelievable creature in the world—if the yeti is but myth —is the gorilla. Isolated bands of these humanoid creatures still exist here and there in the depths of the tropical African jungle.

Particularly since "King Kong" was made, the gorilla has had an undeserved reputation for fierce, dangerous belligerence. Although in captivity he may indeed turn sullen, morose and dangerous, and sometimes even refuse to mate, in the jungle he is the opposite—withdrawn, amiable, timid and shy.

The gorilla band, with as many as thirty members, never leaves its ten-to-fifteen-square-mile home, and although the pygmies and a handful of other African trackers can locate him, he is so self-effacing that others can search for weeks in that small area in vain, or with but a fleeting view of a huge black shadow disappearing into the ferns and bamboo.

However, when his family is faced with real danger, the gorilla's performance lives up to his reputation. The bull stays behind while his females and young flee. He rears on his hind legs to his six-foot height, hair extended on his huge skull, yellow canines bared, blood-shot eyes rolling. He drums reverberatingly on his chest, hoots, roars, hammers the ground berserkly, grasps and shakes trees as if in uncontrollable rage, tearing up and hurling vegetation. If the intruder is not intimidated enough to flee, he makes mock charges, stopping short. The sight of six hundred pounds of furious muscle, capable of crushing most skulls with a listless back-hand swipe, is usually sufficient to rout the most courageous. If not, as a last resort, but only in this extremity, he will charge in earnest. Even then, say scientists who have studied him in his jungle habitat, if a human stands his ground and stares him in the eyes, a bull gorilla will divert his charge at the last moment and slip away into the jungle. So they say. The family is safe by this time anyway, and the bull hurries to catch them, his huge weight on his stocky legs, lightly leaning and balancing on the knuckles of his long arms.

In some ways the gorilla's family life is similar to the

human's. Once formed, the gorilla family stays together for life, although lone bulls may move into the circle for a time for mating, then break off alone again. Young bulls also leave the group with several females to form new family groups. Yet sexual jealousy is rare, the lead bull making no objection if one of the females wishes to mate with another male. But discipline and decisions, such as where to eat and sleep, and what trails to follow, are strictly within the province of the leader. Rollicking juveniles are allowed great latitude, but a cold, glassy stare from under shaggy eyebrows is quickly followed by cracking slaps and cuffs if obedience is not instant.

Other members of the family spread out and search for food only after the bull has stopped traveling and starts eating. The gorilla is a strict vegetarian, existing on bamboo shoots and other bitter vegetation, although in captivity he will eat meat. At twilight, each night in a different place, the gorilla bends down young trees and fronds to form a bed or nest. The young may perch securely in trees, with the females somewhat below them, but the males sleep near the ground. The grunts and high-pitched squeaks—the gorilla has a vocabulary of some twenty sounds—gradually die with the light. As in most families, the young break silence far too early in the white haze of dawn.

Hanno writes of his pre-Christ voyage on this coast: "The second island was full of wild people. By far the greater numbers were women with hairy bodies. Our interpreters called them Gorillas. We gave chase to the men, but could not catch any, for they all scampered up steep rocks and pelted us with stones. We secured three women, who bit and scratched and resisted their captors. But we killed and flayed them, and brought the hides to Carthage." It is not known whether these were a primitive race of pygmies, or a species of chimpanzees, or indeed, gorillas as Hanno wrote.

Far from the coast and forest, at the north end of the microcosm that is the Cameroons—in the Maroua area described by André Gide as "one of the noblest in the world"—lives another people, a shade higher on the evolutionary scale than the pygmies, but somehow seeming less advanced, less self-sufficient, and certainly, less dangerous: the Kirdi.

The Kirdi go clad only in metal bracelets, necklaces and amulets, although the women wear a tiny kirtle strung from the waist. Ceremonial scars circle the nipples of breasts and decorate the cheeks, forehead and chin. Rings puncture single nostrils, or six-inch lip plugs trail from the center of lower lips like straws; pierced ears are strung with elaborate metal earrings; and hair is dyed. They use a few metal spearheads secured at ransom prices from other tribes. In spite of that, this people is still in transition from the Stone Age to the Iron Age.

The tribal groups are patriarchal. The family hierarchy is so strictly delineated that no society, no political or economic organization wider than a family is possible. The head of the family is absolute.

The Kirdi are animists. For them there is but one god, a good god, a god who would never harm poor humans. Therefore, he can safely be ignored—and is. But unfortunately the world is also populated with evil spirits, in the air, the trees, the water, every animate and inanimate object. These evil spirits are insatiable and prey on humans; they must be frequently and recurrently propitiated. The Kirdi lives in constant fear that he is the target for the wrath of some angry, evil god he has forgotten. Before every act he offers sacrifice, such as spilling a drop of water or beer to a god of earth before drinking.

Perhaps it is this habitual fear, perhaps it is their natural dignity, but the Kirdi are one of the kindest and most hospitable people in Africa. Completely unaffected, they still go naked, although in recent years the Government has threatened them with prison if so found on the roads. Coming upon them suddenly, with a piece of cloth or clothing in their hands, they guiltily throw it over a shoulder or around the waist, not knowing just exactly where to put it—or why. But even this vague effort is wasted as the cloth drops to an arm or the ground when they give their hearty handclasp of welcome.

Entering their stone-walled *sares*, perched on rocky

hillsides all around the volcanic scenery near Maroua, one is greeted by the entire family emerging from the round mud huts with conical thatched roofs. One hut larger than the others houses the granaries and the kitchens, one of each for each woman in the family. These granaries are made of baked and burnished clay about ten feet tall with an opening near the top—rats cannot climb that high over the slick finish of the clay. One, a ceremonial granary, is reserved for placing grain offerings to appease the hunger of the spirits.

The host, the head of the family, sends one of his wives, naked except for a leather thong, wiggling head first into the granary opening above to pass down already-cooked sweet potato. The host thumbs off a morsel and eats it to show it is not poisoned, then feeds the earth with a portion, before passing the potato around to his guests.

Outside the windowless hut once again, everyone squats on heels, and the gourd of beer is passed around, after the host wets his lips and spills some to the ground. Native beer all over Africa is the same—the women chew up grain, millet here, and spit it out in a bowl where it ferments till ripe and ready for drinking. The gourd is alive with foreign matter, but no one bothers to shunt the pieces out unless one is so large as to scrape the throat in swallowing. The beer continues fermenting in the belly, and a drunk raised by a day's drinking can continue for a week after the last swallow has been taken. Even the youngest male children have the gourd held for them to drink from, and the guests most of all must tilt the gourd far and often. The adam's apple is watched to judge honesty and courtesy.

Photographing the Kirdi is simple, although the twentieth century has made enough impact to make a small "gift" of coin wildly appreciated even if rarely requested, and the mere sight of a camera sends entire naked villages to line up stiff as ramrods. With foreigners, the Kirdi are like children, friendly, happy, curious, showing wide-eyed amazement at every new sliver of the modern age that penetrates their innocent world.

"Kirdi" means "pagan" in the language of the Foulbes

or Peuls, the Moslem nomads who have crisscrossed this area with their flocks for centuries, so dominating the Kirdi because of superior social organization that they have pushed them from the fertile lowlands to the sterile hills. The Foulbes maintain a strict feudal hierarchy, divided into freemen and serfs, the latter little better than slaves, in which the word of the hereditary chieftain is law. These chieftains live a ceremonial life, surrounded by wives, children and religious aristocracy. The Sultan of Mandera, at Mora near Maroua, has more than forty women in his harem, and uncounted children. He spends his days seated under the trees deliberating before the gate of his rambling mud-walled palace, attended by dignitaries and as many as thirty of his teen-age sons.

On ceremonial occasions, the Sultan is decked out magnificently in rich robes, astride a horse carrying silvered mail and rich silk drapes—and on extraordinary occasions the horse even wears four-legged silk pants reaching to the ground. The Sultan's warriors surround him, armed with swords and lances, strung with all the finery they can muster. When regional meetings of these Moslems are held, as many as five thousand horsemen may gather. Some of the tribes east of Maroua still dress for these ceremonies in chain mail and helmets, centuries old. It is believed this armor is that taken from the bodies of Christian knights of Western Europe by the host of Saladdin in Palestine during the Crusades, centuries ago. It was carried to West Africa by the waves of conquest, fueled by Moslem fervor. The men who own this armor explain simply: "Our fathers gave them to us."

When these desert horsemen gather, hours pass in headlong gallops, lines of horsemen dropping reins to guide with knees only, firing and flipping muskets twisting fifty feet in the air overhead to be caught at full gallop, the line of champing, prancing stallions stopping in a slithering cloud of dust at the very feet of the honored guests.

NIGERIA

Not far from the Atlantic, in the bulge of Africa's western shoulder, a river rises and flows east for over a thousand miles, then turns at ninety degrees to the south, adding fifteen hundred more miles to its long detour before spilling into the Atlantic Ocean.

The sources of this river, the Niger, were known early in the continent's exploration, but the destination of its muddy flood was a mystery.

Leo Africanus drank from the Niger in 1526, in what is today northern Nigeria, and erroneously reported it flowed west. His contemporaries accepted that this meant the Niger was part of the Senegal or Gambia, rivers whose mouths were known. Others for centuries believed the river was a branch of the Nile that flowed from the east across the thirsty Sahara. One speculation held that the Niger flowed into a center lowland of the continent, the sink of Africa, where it was held prisoner, eventually to evaporate and feed the coastal downpours.

The search for the key to the Niger was galvanized by the same intertwining goals as Livingstone's exploration of the Zambezi. A water highway to new inland markets for the products spewed forth by Britain's industrial revolution was needed, and commerce, it was believed, would throttle the slave trade.

But the Niger was a worthy foe. Tenaciously, as if it were indeed the god the animists claim, it clung to its secrets, exacting human sacrifice for each secret bared. For every fifty miles of its serpentine length opened up, at least one life was lost on the altar of Niger.

Major Houghton, the first explorer who cut his way up from the coast, was killed by raiders before he could do more than determine that the river flowed eastward. Seeking to follow up this discovery, Mungo Park, the man who eventually learned more about the Niger than anyone else, led an expedition toward the Niger from Gambia. Park's men deserted him, he was robbed of everything he had, and malaria laid its yellow hand upon him. With imperturbable faith that these disasters and ultimate success were predestined by God, he struggled on, begging food and shelter from Africans, paying for it with the brass buttons from his coat.

In the harem of one local king, the women insisted that both his color and nose were artificial. "The first, they said, was produced when I was an infant, by dipping me in milk; and they insisted that my nose had been pinched every day till it acquired its present unsightly and unnatural conformation." Park in return "praised the glossy jet of their skins, and the lovely depression of their noses; but they said that flattery, or (as they emphatically termed it) honey mouth, was not esteemed . . ."

Park in 1796 finally reached the river with several African travelers. ". . . as I was anxiously looking around for the river, one of them called out, *geo affili* (see the water), and looking forwards I saw with infinite pleasure the great object of my mission—the long sought-for majestic Niger, glittering to the morning sun, as broad as the Thames at Westminster, and flowing slowly to the eastward. I hastened to the brink, and, having drank of the water, lifted up my fervent thanks in prayer to the Great Ruler of all things, for having thus far crowned my endeavors with success."

Park's discovery earned him the backing of the British Government for another expedition, equipped to build a boat and thus travel from the Niger's headwaters to its eventual outlet. He and forty-three others left Gambia for the Niger's headwaters in 1805, but by the time these waters were sighted, thirty-nine of his companions were dead and another insane. Park wrote: ". . . but though all the Europeans who are with me should die, and though I were myself half dead, I would still persevere; and if I could not succeed in the object of my journey, I would at least die on the Niger."

Again, prophetic words from an African explorer. His companions were soon dead and he himself was brutally killed at the Niger's Bussa rapids. Only his African servant survived to carry his papers overland to civilization.

The next expedition attacked by a new route, across the Sahara from Tripoli; two of the three Europeans on this voyage were to be claimed by the Niger. By penetrating as far south as Lake Tchad, they proved the Niger did not run east to the Nile, and by following the river source of Lake Tchad to its swampy beginning only a few hundred miles away, they disproved the African sink theory. The Sultan of Sokoto even told them the Niger did empty into the western ocean, at a port called Rakah.

That was the last success they were to have. One man died there, and the leader, Hugh Clapperton, in an expedition to the coast found no one who knew Rakah. Wearily he trekked back overland, only to die of disease and disappointment, another victim of the Niger. His servant Richard Lander buried him, then tried to follow the Niger to the sea, but he was turned back by hostile natives and forced to return overland to civilization.

Three years later, in 1830, Lander returned with his brother John, and took two canoes down the Niger, from the Bussa rapids where Park had died. Far from the ocean, they were intercepted and captured by King Boy of Brass, a town at the Niger delta. King Boy finally agreed to ransom them to a caravel anchored in the delta, and the war canoes pushed off on the Niger flood again. This seemed the Niger's final insult. Trussed like pigs going to market, the Lander brothers stared in fascination as the secret sought for more than three centuries unfolded before the swift prows, down through the tangled skein of the delta to the sea. The Niger did flow into the Bight of Benin, a theory ancient as the others, but so discredited it had never been tested.

Even then, the discovery of this vast highway to the interior was almost lost again to civilization. Thomas Lake, captain of the ship, haggled over the ransom, but once the Landers were aboard, hoisted anchor and set sail without paying a cent—perhaps the only man in history who cheated the Niger jade of her harshly levied due.

Within two years an attempt was made to use this trade route, the first ocean-going iron vessels, the *Alburkah* and the *Quorra*, steaming up the Niger. But the tiny mosquito stopped the iron boats and sent them fleeing in panic; malaria killed thirty-nine of the forty-eight Europeans on board. In the next twenty years only one other expedition started up the Niger, and nearly half of this group died of malaria. The irony of this voyage was that quinine, the one thing that could have saved many lives, was plentiful in the expedition's stores, but tragically was only administered when a victim had already passed the fever's crux and was recovering.

At the same time trade on the coast expanded, trade that had prospered since the Portuguese explored the Bight of Benin in 1472 and entered the Kingdom of Benin itself in 1486. A member of the expedition, Joham Affom da Aveiro, died there, probably the first on the long casualty list of this country. Before 1500, the King of Benin sent an ambassador to Portugal, and accepted missionaries at his court, ordering a church to be constructed and his son and some nobles to become Christians. Pepper, not only as spice but to preserve meat in the absence of any refrigeration, was the main item of trade—soon abandoned to concentrate on slaving.

In 1553, when Captain Windam of England arrived in Benin, he was astonished to find the King speaking Portuguese, learned as a child. The King promised to fill Windam's ships with peppers in thirty days, and indeed did collect eighty tons, but with his sailors dying like flies of fever, Windam upped anchor in a panic without the pepper, taking away with him only a few barrels of palm oil.

A few years later, a Benin cargo was described as "pepper and elephants teeth, oyle of palm, cloth made from cotton wool very curiously woven, and cloth made from the bark of palm trees." The heavy trade in palm oil, at that time the only suitable ingredient for soap, eventually gave the name "the Oil Rivers" to the channels of the Niger delta, a trade that even today pumps two hundred thousand tons of palm oil a year into tankers in the delta.

The forest kingdom of Benin that the Portuguese and trade opened to the world was started late in the first century, according to legend, and was completely indigenous, unaffected by the Moslem north and at its zenith before contact with Europe.

At that time Benin controlled the Niger delta and the coast all the way into present-day Dahomey. There was no trade without the king's consent, and a standing army of thousands of men enforced his rule. Benin city was defended by heavy walls and surrounded by a moat. Great wealth was amassed from manufacturing and trade, stimulating both a leisure class and a class of artisans. Benin kings were absolute, and an elaborate court ceremony evolved honoring the divinity of the king. Captain Windam noted that subjects cowered on their haunches before the king, covered their eyes so not to look him in the face, and crept backwards from his presence.

As in Uganda, advances in certain fields seemed balanced by regressions in others. Human sacrifice was integral to religion, prisoners, slaves and even tribal members being killed to appease one or another of the four hundred gods worshiped by animists.

Human sacrifice, and slavery, led to the ultimate destruction of Benin Kingdom. In 1897, at the moment of the major Benin feast when tribesmen rededicated themselves to their divine king, a British Consul-General led an armed column to enforce a treaty forbidding the use and sale of slaves, and human sacrifice. This was the moment when the gods forbade strangers to see the king, and demanded greater than usual human sacrifice. Unwilling to anger the British, but religiously bound to continue sacrifice and remain hidden from alien eyes during the feast, the King sent a message to turn back. When the column continued, the consul, five more of the nine Europeans, and most of the two-hundred-man escort were slaughtered by the King's troops.

British retaliation was swift and merciless. The King multiplied sacrifice to ward off the feared punishment. But Benin was stormed and burned, and the King was exiled to Calabar. This was the end of resistance to British rule in southern Nigeria, and the burning city was to be the funeral pyre of a great African kingdom.

Looting the city, the troops carried off twenty-three hundred bronze castings, the Benin bronzes now found in museums throughout the world. These bronzes, some of which were first described by the Moroccan traveler Ibn Battuta in 1353, are in artistry equal to any bronzes ever made. Some are of small groups of figures and bas-reliefs, but a number are busts of kings and their queens. The Benin style, while somewhat formal, is still far more natural than the usual symbolic, fantastic and almost caricaturistic African art. Heavy necklaces, earrings and crowns and elaborate hairdos decorate the busts, and features such as lips, noses and eyes are sculpted in exaggeration, more stylized than natural, all of them instilled with rare grace and movement.

One of the marvels of these bronzes is that such beauty and craftsmanship were obtained with primitive sculpting tools and clay furnaces. The process used has not been used to such perfection since: the Benin artists covered a sculpted clay model with wax, then with potters clay, and then heated the entire assembly to 1050 degrees centigrade until the wax vaporized, filling the slim resultant hollow with molten bronze. Many of these bronzes, some of them recovered from overseas and others dug up in recent excavations, can be seen at the Nigerian Museum in the capital, Lagos.

In spite of Benin's head start, Lagos with its fine harbor soon surpassed the Oil Rivers as principal port. Annexed by England in 1861, long before the rest of the country, it is still the main port, built on three islands and part of the mainland, crowded by half a million people. This is a race of merchants, and every cubbyhole and every person's head is a free enterprise shop—let the buyer beware—and every day is a bustling Christmas shopping day.

Over fifty-five million people, more than a quarter of Africa's population, is crammed into the three hundred fifty thousand square miles of Nigeria, and Lagos seems to be host to members of all two hundred and fifty languages, bridged only by the lingua franca of imperial English.

A skyscraper twenty-five stories high, modern hotels and apartment buildings, a downtown race track, a yachting club at Five Cowrie Shell Creek in mid-town, wide boulevards and mansions all breathe modernity—but it is old Lagos that hypnotizes. A few yards from the principal boulevard, the Marina, along the harbor jammed with international shipping and luxury cruisers, native dugouts glide silently, propelled by a pole in the hands of a man standing in the stern, while another erect in the prow casts his circular butterfly net. Other nets flit out from the wharfs, landing a meal and a sale. At fisherman's wharf, where not more than a hundred years ago palm oil, ivory and slaves were shipped out, a raft of fishing pirogues ties up in the evening, to hang nets from spars, to bake the fresh fish over an open charcoal fire on the decks of pirogues, hurrying before the evening rains, rains that dump twelve or thirteen feet of rain a year on this sweltering malarial coast.

In the eighteenth century, when seven million slaves were shipped to the Americas, mostly Brazil and Cuba, four thousand a year were shipped from this dock in Lagos alone. Even in the nineteenth century, after England had abolished slavery in 1807—and the United States had followed suit in 1808—four million slaves left the west coast, many of them from Lagos. These were mostly prisoners taken in civil wars of the forest kingdoms, wars that annually netted thousands of slaves for sale by the kings to the European slavers.

Oyo was a sister state of Benin, claiming ancestry as did Benin from the parent city of Ife, but separated from the sea by Benin and unaffected by European influence till Lagos assumed great importance. Shortly after Christ, a Christianity leniently adapted to the animist religion was supposed to have migrated from the Middle East to Nigeria. The legend of the founding of Ife, which gave birth to Benin and Oyo, seems to reflect such an influence. The world was pictured as being nothing but water till God sent his son down with a handful of dirt that he sprinkled on the water, a rooster to scratch and fertilize this land, and a palm nut that sprouted into the first tree. The beginning of this life was Ife, from which grew Benin and Oyo.

Oyo's kings were considered semi-divine and exercised absolute power, but were still mortal enough to be responsible to a society of elders. Any excess use of absolute power—especially killings, since blood spilled on the earth was an offense to the god of earth—could prompt the elders to present the king with an empty calabash, intoning "The gods reject you, the people reject you, the earth rejects you." Then the king was obliged to commit suicide.

One of the kings so condemned shot arrows to the

north, south and west and cursed his people before taking his life: "My curse be on you for your disloyalty and disobedience, so let your children disobey you. If ye send them on an errand, let them never return to bring you word again. To all the points I shot my arrows will ye be carried as slaves. My curse will carry you to the sea and beyond the seas, slaves will rule over you, and ye their masters will become slaves." The curse was chillingly fulfilled by the slave raiders who depopulated whole villages of the country.

The fate of another Oyo king was even more bizarre. King Shango was a practitioner of magic, and one day, in perhaps a primitive Benjamin Franklin experiment, he summoned lightning. It destroyed his house and killed most of his wives and children. Shango hanged himself, but ever since has been deified as one of the most important gods in Nigeria, the God of Thunder and Lightning. A statue of this god by the modern Nigerian bronze worker Ben Enwonwu stands menacingly before the Electricity Corporation building on the Marina in Lagos.

As Oyo's rulers grew weaker, former tributaries dared to attack her territory. One of these, Dahomey, had paid yearly to Oyo forty men, forty women, forty guns and four thousand loads of cowrie shells, but finally revolted. An army of sixteen thousand, led by six thousand amazons, excess wives of the king of Dahomey, attacked the town of Abeokuta. The town was on the verge of surrendering when the insulting realization that they were faced by women stiffened the defenders' resistance. With the aid of Europeans in the town who gave ammunition and advice, they finally drove the amazons off.

One of these Europeans was a Baptist missionary named Bowen who had previously fought in the American Indian wars at the side of Davy Crockett. Another American active in these local wars was named Pettiford, an expert rifleman who was used to pick off enemy chiefs during battle.

Little is known of Ife, the spiritual home of Oyo and Benin, but it has given the world another series of bronzes, many of which were discovered only in 1938. These Ife bronzes, cast hundreds of years before the Benin bronzes, are completely naturalistic, somehow even more fragile and airy than the Benin pieces. Although one or two of these are displayed at the Lagos museum, the most complete collection is in the small museum at Ife itself.

These Ife bronzes in turn have their roots in a culture that flourished in central Nigeria from about 900 B.C. till several centuries A.D., a culture called the Nok. Nok sculpture is in terra cotta, fragile, two-thousand-year-old masterpieces of naturalism that have survived the vicissitudes of destruction of their civilization and burial to a depth of thirty feet. These sculptures were only discovered in 1936, scattered about the village of Nok, a small village near the mountain rest center of Jos in north central Nigeria. The majority of Nok pieces are displayed at the small Jos museum, which also displays an original example of twentieth-century sculpture from America—a Model T Ford.

Jos is a comfortable African resort with all amenities, and a rainbow of temperate-zone flowers coiled and draped loosely around comfortable colonial buildings. But a mile from the outskirts, Africa thrusts harshly into the conscious again.

Nothing grows in the dry season. The arid plateau and jumbled granite hills are gray. Capricious erosion has perched silk-slick boulders in defiance of gravity on sheer granite slopes. Parched trees and brush crevice the rock with their thirsty roots, the whole a surrealistic mobile from a dead planet. This dull world is shockingly ripped open, raped, by the obscene splashes of orange sherbet, large and profuse blossoms, that incomprehensibly find glowing life at the end of lifeless-looking branches when water has become a mere memory. The bush is burned here, as all over Africa, to fight back the ever encroaching shrubs and let the grasses breathe and grow. Raging brush fires mushroom billowing clouds of smoke and soot to block out the gray, orange and blue of the horizon.

This is the land of the Jerawa tribe, numerically one of the smallest remaining in Africa. Jerawa women are the duckbills, the platterlips. In their childhood, upper and lower lips, and sometimes even both ear lobes, are pierced. Once the bloody spurt is staunched with herbs and healing

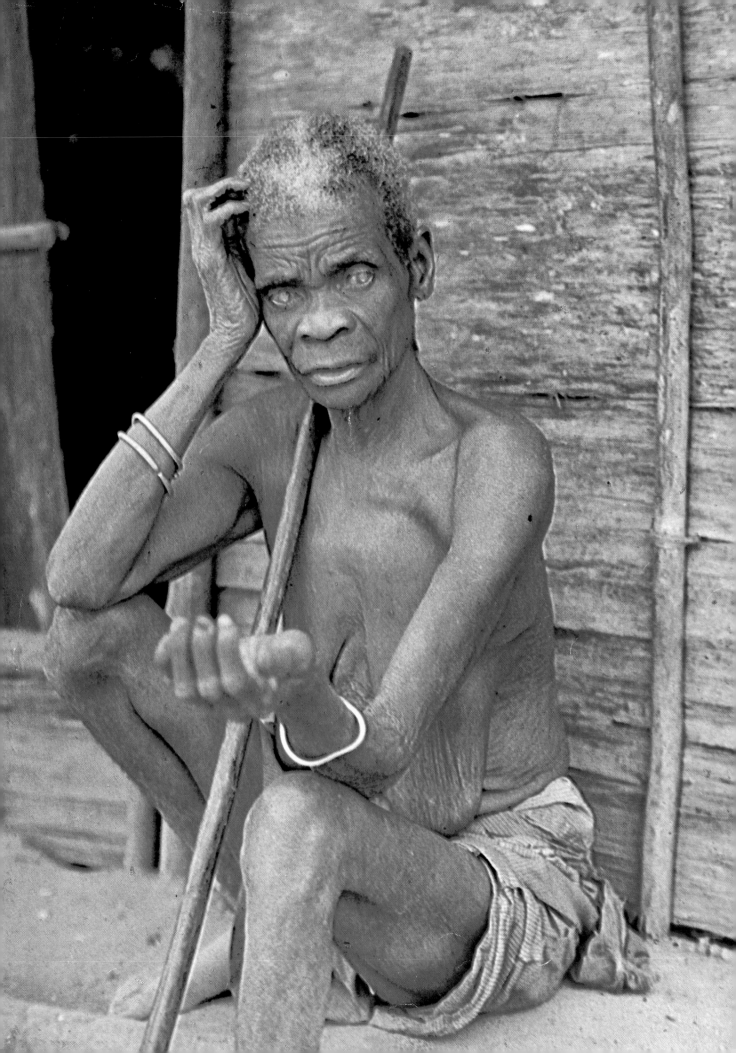

sets in, plugs of ivory or wood are forced into the wounds. As the sensitivity of lips lessens, these plugs are enlarged periodically, stretching and enlarging the lips until death.

The males of the tribe are completely undistinguished, and one immediately wonders what powers they possess to inflict this form of "beauty" on their women. Some interpret this mutilation as a defensive measure of a small, weak tribe against more powerful neighbors to keep the women from being kidnapped by making them so unattractive they are unwanted. If true, the defense has succeeded admirably.

The distended lips bare both upper and lower teeth as well as the gums in a grimace. A perpetual whinny of a horse comes to mind immediately. Other than this decoration of plugs, they are completely nude, except for an ineffectual braid of vines and leaves picked fresh each morning. A black headdress of mud and ashes, much like a skullcap or inverted bowl, is worked into and covers the hair, chunks of it cracking after a few weeks and exposing the black curls underneath. Implausibly, the question of how these women would eat an apple—nonexistent in this wilderness—tickles the curiosity. The simple answer is disappointing. For eating and sleeping, the plugs are slipped out, and the muscle-less, stretched flesh flaps uncontrollably.

The traveler finds his reverie on this monstrous deformation interrupted when these grotesque women laugh boisterously—at him and his sport shirt and shorts—a somewhat painful pleasure for them.

Centuries ago, this province was part of the Kingdom of Zazzau, one of the seven Hausa states that spread over most of northern Nigeria. The warrior queen Bakwa Burunku who ruled Zazzau early in the fourteenth century had two daughters during her thirty-year reign, Amina and Zariya. According to legend, Zariya was espoused to a local chief, but became bored and left her husband to found a new city called Zaria, followed there shortly thereafter by her lonesome husband. Amina, jealous of this new queen, took the throne of Zazzau from her mother and set out to conquer her world. In each town she captured, she took a

lover, a lover to whom she remained faithful till she abandoned the town, when she personally sacrificed him, so that he could never love another woman.

The history of Zazzau and the other Hausa states is perhaps better known than the history of most of Black Africa, since the Moslem religion early introduced the written word, and thousand-year-old records have survived, such as the Chronicle of the city of Kano.

Bayajidda, son of the King of Bagdad, founded the Hausa states in the first century A.D., according to tradition. Because of a quarrel with his father, Bayajidda traveled to Africa, finally arriving at the city of Daura. In Daura he slew a snake that had prevented people from drawing water from the community well, whereupon the Queen of Daura married him. Their six grandsons founded other Hausa states.

These states were oriented to the north, to the Sahara, to the camel caravans that traversed the endless sands, then along the North African littoral all the way to Cairo and on to Bagdad. Each city-state had a duty. Gobir defended against raids from the empires of Mali and Songhai in the north. Daura was the spiritual capital. Katsina—and to some extent Kano—was the terminus for the caravan trade. To the south, Zazzau was the slave raider against the forest kingdoms, and Rano and Biram with Kano produced the dyed cotton, the iron and the leather for trade.

Today a jet airport and a modern city of wide boulevards surround the ancient walled city, and though the arched gates are intact, the walls have crumbled to form a fifteen- to twenty-foot-high regular hill, and it is invaded by rubber-tired wagons and even cars. Yet basically it is the same. Once inside its gates, a thousand years drop from the calendar.

This is the center of another world, a Saharan world, a Moslem world without Arabs, with black rather than Semitic faces, the commercial center of the universe where everything is for sale, and everyone is selling some part of that everything. Each corner, each minuscule shop, almost each inch, is a market in itself. Buyer and seller mingle with sheep and goats, all wandering aimlessly, the latter filching free lunch from baskets of peanuts, carrots or flour. Sugar cane, bananas, oranges, twenty-foot-long python skins, wooden carvings, occasional Nok figurines, crocodile bags and skins, mammy cloth, antimony and other cosmetics, jewelry, myriads of spices, beckoning from afar with scents out of a Thousand and One Nights, Maria Theresa silver dollars, clay bricks, boards—everything is here.

A native guide is necessary; not to see the sights but for protection, protection from the hordes of ubiquitous children, paralyzed with outstretched arm, except for strident voices screaming a litany of "gimme dash," or those with a French tendency, "dash-moi." Dash is the international lubricant.

Even these children are merchants. All of them, especially the girls, seem to carry baskets of any salable item on their heads, a sort of natural model school that betrays the origin of their extremely upright, sergeant-major posture and slinky grace. Even from eight or nine years old, the majority of these girls use antimony mascara, wear a sort of lipstick, and have their faces powdered. They must have sisters, older sisters, and the traveler begins to long to see them. But the traveler does not see them, ever. Purdah reigns over Kano, and all women of marriageable age are confined to their homes, at least until that age when it seems to make no difference, when the young girls in the street are balanced by the very elderly who are only distinct by their complete lack of appeal.

A Westerner finds this purdah, the veiling and confining of the young women and wives, to be a somewhat amusing version of cutting the nose off to spite the face. Rare is the home that has water in it, and since the women cannot be seen on the street or at the community wells, the husband becomes the scrubwoman, thousands of them rub-a-dubbing the weekly laundry in the water holes, exchanging gossip like any good hausfrau. The ancient war gods of Kano must blush.

When the Emir—the descendant of the King of Kano —is in town, his bodyguard in brightly hued dress mans the main gate of the huge mud-walled conglomeration of buildings known as the castle. Hundreds of people wait under

the grilling sun merely for a glimpse of the Emir or to request justice for a petition. Overlooking this open-air court is the great mosque, intrinsically of little interest because of its modern construction, but slimly beautiful for its twin towers that look at Kano from the same height as the endless circle of vultures.

Like Cairo, Kano too has its pyramids. Only the pyramids of Kano stretch for acres—acres of pyramids of peanuts. Called groundnut here, the peanut is prolific, over-taxing the facilities of the one-track railroad to the ocean. Impossible to ship, the peanuts are stored in seven-hundred-ton pyramids, dismantled according to age and as the single track can accommodate them.

Kano is more than a market. It is a factory. An open-air factory. This is the home of indigo blue, the burnished blue cloth that gave a name to a race, the Tuaregs. These are the "blue men," the desert nomads who roam from southern Morocco to southern Libya, the race of Moslems whose women are not veiled but whose men are, and all of whom are literally blue, blue from the transfer of the indigo dye from the cloth to their skins after years of dressing in this cloth. At the dye pits—unchanged in two millennia in place and method—the workers are also blue, blue from working the indigo. The dirty-white cotton is hand dipped into clay pits filled with the indigo solution.

Absorbing successive dippings, the cloth shades from a dull to an iridescent green, from sky-blue to the dark royal purple of the dyed but unfinished cloth. After drying on lines in the oven-like air, the cloth goes to the beating huts. In these circular mud-thatched huts many two-man teams beat the cloth to render it smooth and gleaming, almost a silken or satin sheen. Pieces of hardwood, looking like nothing more than small fireplace logs with handles, are used to beat repeatedly every square inch of the cloth draped across a supporting log. When handed one of these hammers, even the athletic traveler feels a sudden weakness in the wrist and finds the weight pulling his arm straight down. Yet these indigo beaters flay away at the cloth with rapid continuous left and right hand strokes for ten or twelve hours a day without apparent effort, rippling symphonies of muscle.

Next to the dye pits, the stench is worse, overpowering. Thousands of skins—cattle, goat, sheep, snake, crocodile, antelope and even camel—are treated at the tanning factory. Scrapers working over skins stretched on small logs shear away the body fat down to the outer skin with instruments that look like ancient planers. The skins are then rubbed endlessly with curing chemicals, before time and sun are allowed to take over and complete the tanning process, loosing upon unsuspecting nostrils a devil's brew of hideous odors. One of the resulting tanned skins is Moroccan leather, produced here but named long ago after the craftsmen who tooled it in that Cherifian kingdom to the north.

All these skins are native produce, even the python skins. North and east of Kano, the python breeds in abundance, living in dens deep in the dark earth. The python's skin is valuable, and he is hunted. It is easy to find his field of multiple holes and dens, and for the natives of this area it is even easy to tell by smell which den harbors these painted tubes of muscle.

But the ancient method of hunting the python, effective as it may be, is today rarely pursued. Infrequently, it is demonstrated for special friends. Once the den where the python lurks is determined, the hunter heavily greases a leg, then squats over the hole. Gingerly the greased leg is extended down the den, the other leg and arms braced against the edges. Once the python tries to swallow the leg, the tug of war is irreversibly engaged. The hunter is securely braced and his body too large to be pulled into the hole. The snake cannot egorge the leg and peristalsis literally pulls him out of his den. Slowly the python head inches up to the surface, toothless jaws distended over thigh, eyes blindly bulging in helpless muscular reaction, a captive of gluttony. Strong fingers grasp the patterned head, ruthless knife slits from jaw to gullet, and the threshing body is pulled reluctantly from the grease on the black leg. Another skin is chucked on the swelling pile.

IVORY
COAST

weeping in from the vacant miles of the South
Atlantic, thousands of years of sea and surf have
tossed up high sand bars—almost barrier reefs—
along the Ivory Coast, sand bars that have become islands,
half a mile wide and a hundred and fifty miles long, curved
palms marching up to the steep beach, peppered with
rattan cottages, restaurants and fishing villages.

To the leeward of the bar, hidden and protected from
the sea, are the lagoons, natural waterways sometimes
several miles wide, interlocked by canals. They form an
inland waterway of calm transportation and fishing some
two hundred and fifty miles long. The pirogues glide
silently here, one man poling while the other flips a pebble
into the still water to attract hungry fish, sailing out his
hawk net to settle tangling about his prey. On the wind-
ward side of the reef, whole villages toil.

Standing on a log five feet in diameter and thirty feet
long, a dozen ax wielders systematically hew it into a high-
prowed ocean-going pirogue. The blue nets are spread to
dry nearby, gnarled-fingered fishermen mending the torn
seines. Crews with their pirogues brave the heavy surf,
first starting high on the beach, standing like statues as
they read the waves. Suddenly, without a word, as if moved
by the same set of muscles, they slip the pirogue forward
and down the wet shore, leap in and paddle furiously to
cross the trough before the next wave breaks in ten-foot-
tall showers of foam. Slipping a net over the gunwale behind them, they paddle a long arc, dropping the net as they
go, coming in again to ride the crest of thundering surf
perfectly to a soughing beaching on the rippled sand. Eager
village hands, young and old, grab the net's two ends and
the backbreaking tug of war with the pulsing ocean starts
as the net is laboriously hauled in inch by inch, hand over
hand, till the leaping silver harvest cascades onto the
golden sand, seized, gutted and tossed aside to dry in the
sun.

Built on a series of peninsulas jutting into the lagoon
from the mainland, and sprawling onto the barrier island,
mushrooms Abidjan, the capital of the Ivory Coast, Pearl
of the Lagoons. Founded only in 1904 as a railhead, as was
Nairobi, the city has tripled in size to more than three

hundred thousand since the Vridi canal was cut through the barrier island in 1950, enabling ocean-going vessels to dock in the lagoons. A boom town, the city is graced with luxury hotels boasting swimming pools—and one hotel flying in T-bone steaks from Texas—restaurants featuring food from every continent, flower-packed parks, a grandiose four-million-dollar presidential residence and exciting night life.

The African quarters of Adjame and Treichville pump the throb into Abidjan life. Their markets are perhaps more swollen and frantic than most markets in Africa— mask and votive wood carvings, bows and arrows, daggers, drums, patterned black and brown Katiola pottery. Orange-blossomed night breezes tempt the exotic. The heat sends the entire population to perch on stoops, and one bongo beat on a corruguated iron wall or a taut drumskin spills a writhing mass of humanity into the narrow streets, erupting into spontaneous music and endless dance. The moon rises the second time before the thrum of insect host vibrates louder than the weary, fading, final tentative taps on the drumheads. Sleep, Treichville.

Back of Abidjan and the lagoons, away from the sea, silent as Treichville at murky dawn, stretches the rain forest—Tarzan's jungle—swathing the black earth in a muffler of green over most of the Ivory Coast. Silent, deadly, imperturbable. At its edge where slanting sunbeams nourish it, the forest is impenetrable, a woven mat of rampant verdure. From the air it is a lifeless green carpet, woof and warp tufted indiscriminately here and there by emergent giants. No sign of life. Once past the defensive tangle of its edge, it is dead and decayed, permanent shadow, continual chill, a sickening, moldering odor. Only the trunks, heavy root-ribbed pillars, loom in the gloomy vacuum. High above, sixty to a hundred feet, the first branches intercept the vertical columns, interstices of a smothering vaulted roof. Lianas leap to the green roof —how else could they touch sky from the humus-heaped floor—and here and there a strangler vine clings cloyingly to the putrescent decay of a dead host with its braided death-hug, a hollow, leafless, tendrilless twist of stalk, struggling to the light.

Between the dungeon dearth of life in the airless twilight zone and the expressionless upper quilt spread under the sun, there is a hidden but lively world. Birds in clouds, monkeys in chattering waves, and parasitic hundred-hued flowers bask in the light, live and die far above, falling for the first time to the dank embrace of the fetid humus when withering death cuts them down. All this living and dying passes unseen by the diminutive figure of man on the jungle floor.

This hundred thousand square miles of forest is populated by six hundred different branches of the tree family. One species has only three living members in the Ivory Coast, each separated from the other by one hundred and fifty miles. The mechanics of such erratic and spare reproduction are an enigma. As Huxley said, man and forest are natural enemies, and nowhere does man feel safe in it except for the tamed timber regions in some temperate zones of Europe and America.

Man is attacking this jungle, however, farming it for lumber. The felling of the forest mahoganies, sambas and other commercial hardwood giants is spectacular. A crew may work all day on one tree, perched on staves driven into the trunk above the root ribs fifteen to twenty feet from the ground, gnawing at it for hours before the first ominous creak is heard. A shiver shakes the trunk. Loggers scurry down and scatter to safety. Slowly, reluctantly, sinews screeching in protest, the giant that was a sapling when the first Portuguese walked this coast topples with a crash that seems to jar the entire forest, punching an obscene hole in the green tent above. Cut into manageable lengths, these trees are floated down river during the rainy season to the lagoons, where in the Abidjan harbor they join huge log rafts, waiting to be loaded on ships bound for European sawmills.

Some of the rarest game in Africa exists in this equatorial forest, the pygmy hippo and the dwarf elephant and buffalo, but glimpses of them in this Stygian gloom are more rare than they are themselves.

In these forests one also finds the mamba. Poisonous—as indeed all African snakes seem to be—green or black in the same family, the mamba, only as thick as a man's thumb, reaches ten to twelve feet in length. It rears up, five and six feet into the air, on its back quarters, to pursue even a running man, and strike at the head and neck. Death is quick, three minutes at the most. Mambas caught by surprise by approaching cars, have been known to rear up and attempt to strike in the window. Their most chilling trait is their reputed loyalty to their life-long mate—if one of a pair is killed, the other seeks or trails the body, supposedly stalking and striking anyone who foolishly dares to keep the skin.

As in nearly all West Africa, the most interesting denizens of this tropical jungle are the people themselves, over one hundred tribes in small Ivory Coast alone. Other than a few polished stone axes, little is known of the early inhabitants here, though there is a persistent native tradition that their ancestors were a race of small people, a tradition seemingly corroborated by the small-sized, but not pygmy, Gagou tribe thriving in the heart of the Ivory Coast.

The first outsiders to touch the coast were the Portuguese, in the fifteenth century, during Henry the Navigator's lengthy push toward the Cape of Good Hope. French missionaries established a post at Assaine in 1687. At that time the Ivory Coast was known variously as the Gold Coast, the Coast of Good People, the Coast of Teeth, Coast of Males, Coast of Seeds, and other names descriptive of trade. There has never been much ivory in this country, and ivory carving has only started recently under the impetus of the tourist trade.

Although a colony of France, the Ivory Coast was not pacified and the people more or less disarmed till just before the First World War. The last tribal leader to resist was Samory, a former slave who traded and fought at the side of his European master, then, as the head of his tribe, entered the slave trade on his own. He resisted the French successfully for sixteen years, till he was finally captured in 1913 at Man in western Ivory Coast.

Neither French Christianity from the coast nor the Moslem faith from the interior affected these Africans much, and today more than 70 per cent of the population is still animist. One area, in the northeast near Bouna Forest

Reserve, still has much of its late Stone Age character. It is inhabited by the Lobi, an archaic tribe similar to the Kirdi in the Cameroons. Nearly naked, they live in a *soukala*, a primitive earthen fortress that houses an entire family, including its livestock. The men still cling to the bow and arrow, expert in the use of this silent weapon. The women insert plugs of stone or wood in their lips and carry their babies in woven baskets on their backs. They use cowrie shells for currency.

In the area of Man, where Samory was captured, many tribes have retained their ancient customs. Man is the center of the only mountainous area of the Ivory Coast—the rest of the country mounting steadily from the sea to a plateau only a thousand feet high—and is surrounded by twenty-two mountains, Mount Nimba being the highest at 5340 feet. The tribes here—as in most of the country—practice circumcision and excision, elaborate ceremonies at pubescence heavily laden with religious import. Dancing, sometimes performed by the entire village, at other times by specialized dance teams, is integral to these rituals, and to nearly all other facets of tribal activity, since life is so continually dependent on the favor of the many gods.

Although some of these dances are secret, there are many that the traveler can arrange to see. In Man, to the beat of tom-tom, heavily masked and disguised men dance intricately on stilts twenty feet tall, the stilts covered with long trousers so that the dancers assume the aspect of giants, able to communicate with the powerful gods they honor. At Biankouma in the hills near Man, boys, the future hunters, stalk game rhythmically; the antelope's ears prick, he hesitates, then springs off; the hunters find the spoor and excitement mounts as antelope tires and hunters close . . . a bow string twangs, the antelope leaps for sky, rattles and drums pace his pierced heart pumping out red blood to the black soil, hunters unleash a frenzy of stomping joy.

There are fire dances, and even snake dances. The Medy dancers are famed for their acrobatic dances. Near Man and Danane, thirty miles away, one can see the dance of the virgins. Naked from the waist up—except when outsiders watch, when they don shawls for brassieres and con-

tinually fuss and flutter at the irritating encumbrance—
these girls sway through the oldest dance of all, the search
for a mate. Movements that would be lascivious on a
burlesque stage remain knowing but innocently natural to
these forest nymphs. The traveler lucky enough to be
singled out by one of them for her dance leaves with no
doubt she will find her mate.

Danane is also known for its great market, where all
dress in riotous colors and a rainbow would seem pale.
Eight miles on a forest track from Danane, the liana
bridge of Drongouineu stretches across the Cavally River.
Drongouineu and one other liana bridge offer the only
bridging of the Cavally, and have been in use for years. It
is forbidden to wear footwear while crossing this span—
perhaps originally because bare feet gave surer balance on
a swaying bridge, but now a custom sanctified through
decades of tradition to a religious taboo.

Farther along the Cavally from Danane dwell the
juggler dancers. Before these dancers are ready they take
hours in elaborate religious ceremonies of dressing and
ritualistic painting of their bodies. The dancers—several
girls under ten, and half a dozen muscular men—carry
fetishes of leopard skins and stuffed rat or ground squirrel
skins. The girls, expressionless and seemingly hypnotized
by the drums, are "immunized" against harm by rubbing
their bodies with the fetishes, care being taken not to smear
the ritual body paint. Extremely supple, they are bent into
contortionist positions, twirled in the air, through the
legs, around the back, and even grasped by hands and
ankles while the male dancers "skip rope" with their bodies,
all to the heavy beat on the hollow log. In the culminating
act, the leader drapes a girl across his forearms, each of his
hands holding a short, heavy sword. He flips the girl in a
twirl high in the air, stretching the swords full length
above him and actually touching her stomach with their
tips as she falls spinning back toward the ground and into
his arms, unharmed as sword points are turned at the last
instant, flipped up again and again until the sweat pours
from his ebony body—and from the forehead of the spec-
tator, who is fearfully certain the next spinning drop will
plunge a sword into the taut belly.

SIERRA
LEONE

On a Freetown market day, vendors and their wares arrive from Sierra Leone's mainland across white-capped sea of the harbor in schools of native sailboats, packed dangerously close to shipping water. The craft sail out of the rough water and approach the sand beach at the edge of King Jimmy's wharf, coming to by collapsing the sail; even the hinged mast topples into the water with the butt resting on board.

Brawny stevedores carry women passengers and fragile produce in their arms—and some men on their backs—the twenty yards to shore, while knotted clumps of yams, baskets, packs of skins, and stalks of green bananas are tossed into the water to be wafted ashore by the gentle waves. Buyers and relatives eagerly line the water's edge —some of them lifting skirts and wading out—and a cacophony of greetings and cries in a dozen languages adds to the market's din. The market spreads along the wharf and up the Portuguese steps in color-saturated bustle. The newcomers elbow and hip an opening, stretch ground cloths, spread their wares and add to the bedlam with their hawking cries.

King Jimmy's wharf, named after a local king who ruled when Freetown was founded, has seen many great captains. Hanno is thought to have watered here in the sixth century B.C. Thirty years before Columbus sailed, a Portuguese sailor, Pedro da Cintra, wetted anchor and named the country "Mountains of the Lion." The notorious young slaver Sir John Hawkins ravaged the area in 1564. Sir Francis Drake on the last lap of his voyage around the world carved his name on a stone here in 1579, as did the Dutch Admiral Ruiter during his war on English bases in 1664.

This harbor at Freetown is attractive to any ship, being the third largest natural harbor in the world. During World War II three hundred ships at one time, including the Queens Mary and Elizabeth, sought protective anchorage here. The shelter proved ineffective for some; their coral-encrusted hulks furnish caves for the teeming fish, superstructures sending rusted arms through the lapping waves to entreat the heavens where the bombers have disappeared. One of them lies on the outskirts of Freetown a few yards off Lumley beach, sixty miles of beach with white, hard-packed sand so finely ground it gives off a cornstarch creak under bare feet. Marlin up to two thousand pounds are caught near the wreck.

Freetown was founded and named by slaves from the Americas freed and returned to Africa. The effects of Freetown's arbitrary history are easily observed today. Many of the recaptives—as the freed slaves were called—were named by missionaries or selected their own new names, and their descendants, known as Creoles, have completely Anglo-Saxon family and first names. York, Waterloo, Wellington, Kent and Hastings, quarters of the town, were named by British soldiers or sailors who pensioned out here after the anti-slavery blockade. Even the lingua franca of the country is a mixture of English and native words, called krio or creole.

The blood here, starting with the first colony of freed slaves who were accompanied by English women, is perhaps more mixed than in any other country, including the United States. All shades of color are seen on the streets. The architecture is quite as eclectic, African, European and American. Jarringly, because of the annual torrential rains of up to seventeen feet, practical, water-resistant but ugly corrugated iron is used extensively. London-style double-decker buses give the final touch.

The founding of Freetown and Sierra Leone was the culmination of a cycle started in 1441, half a century before Columbus sailed. A Portuguese ship was picking its way along the coast of Morocco in search of hides and oil. As recorded in Portuguese chronicles, the young captain, Antam Gonçalvez, felt that in addition to trading, "O how fair a thing it would be . . . to bring the first captives before the face of our Prince." Gonçalvez accomplished his "fair thing." His men spear-wounded and captured a man, as well as a "Black Mooress," and brought them to the court of King Henry the Navigator.

This skirmish was the first recorded time that captives from Black Africa were taken by Europeans, the first captives that were to swell into the multi-million-man Atlantic slave trade. The number of slaves taken from Africa in the four centuries of slaving that followed will never be accurately known. Figures accepted most frequently cite twenty-four million shipped to the Americas from the west coast of Africa alone. Probably no more than fifteen million of these survived the six-week-long infamous Middle Passage across the Atlantic, eating nothing but yams, chained and packed so tight between decks they only had a foot of sitting space per person, and as little as eighteen inches of headroom. Bodies were jettisoned daily.

Such execrable conditions, enforced by a belief common among west coast Africans that whites were cannibals and were to boil them down for oil or eat them, led to frequent no-quarter revolts. One was recorded on the *Don Carlos* in 1700. Armed with knives, pieces of iron torn from a forecastle door, broken shackles and clubs, the slaves attacked the armed crew, killing several before being beaten back, "and many of the most mutinous leapt overboard, and drown'd themselves in the ocean with much resolution, shewing no manner of concern for life."

Only thirty years after America was discovered, the first slave revolt occurred on the island of Hispaniola, and from then on they broke out constantly all over the New World. As early as the seventeenth century runaway slaves in Jamaica had formed their own nation. When the American revolution broke out in 1776, Britain promised freedom to all American slaves who would fight with England. Many did, and after the war eleven hundred were settled in Nova Scotia, and another fifteen hundred taken to England. The right of such men to remain forever free once they touched British soil had been won in a court case in 1772 by the abolitionist Granville Sharp.

Sharp finally persuaded the Government to send the freed slaves—penniless and unhappy in the frigid climate —to a new tropical home in their native Africa. The first four hundred and eleven, freed slaves and eighty English women, landed in Sierra Leone in 1787, completing the cycle started by Gonçalvez. In 1794 the eleven hundred freed slaves from Nova Scotia arrived, and in 1795, the Maroons, the descendants of the slaves who had formed a free nation in the mountains of Jamaica. They had finally surrendered to the Jamaican government after a hundred years of rebellion, out of fear of the savage dogs introduced to track them.

In 1807 Britain outlawed slavery, followed by the United States in 1808. In the next five years over six thousand slaves were rescued by the British blockade and set free in Freetown, and others were repatriated after slave revolts in Brazil and Cuba. Even then recaptives were not beyond the dangers of slavery. In 1840 alone, over fifteen hundred of them were killed or enslaved in civil wars. Some recaptives, in spite of the horrors they had suffered, dealt in slaves themselves, sending thousands to the fate they had escaped.

The Atlantic slave trade was finally ended during the American Civil War when Union ships aided the British in the anti-slave patrol on the high seas. The last interception of a loaded slaver took place in 1863. Of the three hundred and sixty-eight slaves on board, one hundred and twenty died before they could be landed in Freetown. The last two slavers were seized, empty, in 1864— as the blockade tightened, slavers took to throwing chained captives overboard at the approach of a patrol ship.

Even then, Freetown was not done with slavery. In 1927, Britain learned that domestic slavery was still widely practiced in Sierra Leone. The consequent public outcry forced a new law through Parliament that finally crushed the practice.

Beside the predominantly Christian Creole world of Sierra Leone, there are the Africans native to the country. The two have never melded well. Prominent in this other world are the secret societies, which control tribal life. Little is known of them except for their public exhibition of dancing given at the end of the period of seclusion for initiates. Music rings through Freetown and the other towns nearly nightly, drums announcing such public exhibitions. The Wunde society teaches bravery and endurance of pain, and exotic dancing replete with spectacular costumes, singing and drumming. The Gola and Porro societies demonstrate their acrobatic agility and physical strength in their dances, while the Sande society is reserved for women singers and dancers. One member of the Sande, Madame Yoko, Queen of Senehun—much like a modern movie star—decided she had attained the pinnacle of wealth, love and honor, so she committed suicide with poison, rather than grow old and ugly and be supplanted by another.

For this animist world the Nomoli are gods of fertility. These are male or female seated figures with bulbous features, rough-carved from soapstone. They were created at least six hundred years ago, although not even the local animists can tell their exact origin and date. Found in the earth by farmers, they are now kept in little thatched shelters, worshiped and offered sacrifices of rice. In return, they are expected to steal off in the night and pilfer healthy plants from other farms. If a crop is bad, the Nomoli has failed in his duty. He is removed from his shelter and flogged—a true flagellation ceremony—and the animist farmer confidently expects the Nomoli will perform better for next year's crop.

SENEGAL

The first European contacts with Black Africa, those first sliver-wedges in the cracks that eventually pried open the continent for conquest, more often than not took place on coastal islands—such as Freetown, Grand Bassam, Lagos, Zanzibar and Mombasa.

No mystery this: captains of the frail barques skidding precariously before unknown winds through uncharted waters found the islands godsends of haven, to replenish water, repair ship's planking and sail, and, most of all, defend against the hostile mainland reception so frequently awaiting the white intruder.

Such was Goree, a speck of rock less than twenty-seven hundred yards square. Gateway to Senegal and one of the first pricks in Africa's green wall, Portuguese boots first trod there in 1444, when Denis Dias swung his caravel into the little harbor on the leeward side. Hanno had passed two thousand years earlier, but no record of a landing exists. The greeting for the first landing party to the mainland three miles away was usual—a hail of arrows and spears.

The Dutch took over from the Portuguese, establishing a permanent slaving post there in 1617. They named the island, possibly after a Dutch town, or more disturbingly, after the breaking pole, the *goree,* which savagely lashed two slaves together till pain dictated docility. Or, judging by the heavy traffic in slaves from Goree, this wooden cross of slavery may have been invented on or named after the island itself.

Morbidly, one of the main attractions on the island today is the Slave House. Its cornerstone was laid the year of America's independence. For nearly a century after, it housed slaves till they could be shipped to America. At first the slaves were auctioned in the local market, then marched over the jetty to be stowed into the cramped holds of slave ships. When secrecy became necessary to escape the tightening British blockade of slave ships, a Slave House door that opened directly on the sea was used at night to send slaves by lighter to the ocean-anchored ships. Today, from the sand street, through the door in the outer wall, one can see through the Slave House directly to the sea door, the last view of their continent for thousands of Africans. Two symmetrical staircases arch from the ground over the passage to the sea, up to the slave master's ample living quarters. Flanking the ground passage through the House, small, dank slave dungeons, lit by narrow wall slits, depress the spirit even now. Standing on the surf-splattered sill of the ocean door, the haze and fog offshore readily conjure up the backward-rolling eyes, the frantic muscles forced against rigid shackles, the oath and slap of cat-o'-nine, the final debilitating death of hope, the curse of a heart that beats when willed to fail.

Slaving center and trading post, port of call on all voyages along the west coast, a pawn in international commerce and politics, Goree was conquered and reconquered by the Portuguese, Dutch, English and French till the Treaty of Versailles gave it to the French. Relics of this roisterous past dot the island. There are Portuguese, Dutch and French forts, the latter armed right up to the Second World War. Littering streets, half buried all over the island, and rusting or wallowing in the surf that carves the island's volcanic basalt pillars into organ pipes, a host of iron and bronze cannon spiked by Time trumpet this martial history. On the crown of the island, goats seek sparse grazing beside turret-mounted long cannon that dueled with German dreadnoughts. Beneath the granite cap, rusting tracks scurry along tunnels that once shunted ammunition and guns to the windows in the island's cliffs overlooking the sea. Discarded cannon lie below in the green water.

War is obsolete on Goree. Peace is omnipresent. No wheels—not car nor bicycle—are allowed on the island. There are no sidewalks and no paved streets, just sandy pedestrian thoroughfares, house to house carpets of muffling sand. The sand-washed homes seem transported from the Riviera, a two-story geometry of rose and yellow ocher, tightly packed, shaded by tropical softwoods and ineffectual baobabs.

During the winter months, when sardines bank in the cold currents offshore, feeding fish chase them in great schools to the shallow waters off the island, where they huddle for days in terror. Women and children, naked from the waist up, exhaust themselves scooping out quicksilver torrents of sardines into swamping pirogues or onto rocky beaches. Lobsters grow to fifteen pounds in these waters, and spear fishing in the transparent depths is too easy to be a sport.

Goree's peace is partially the price paid for progress; the capital is now Dakar across the bay on the mainland, sheltered by the snout-nosed peninsula of Cape Vert. Skyscrapers, glass-walled villas and modernistic government edifices line flowered boulevards, while rubbing elbows with jerry-built shops, thatched huts and broad acres of markets. This metropolis of half a million dwindles to sand and baobab, and Senegal stretches flat to the horizons beyond its borders. Only the Phare des Mamelles, Lighthouse of the Breasts, tipping one of a pair of hills on the outskirts of town, breaks the flat expanse of Senegal, its exclamation point of light marking the western-most landfall of Africa, Almadies Point, a finger of land and submerged shoals pointing at Brazil three thousand miles away.

North, where the peninsula ends and the land turns so the heavy waves once again strike straight at the shore, a medieval fishing village sends its huts staggering along the sand. Kayar. Dawn glinting from the sand into the towering waves finds the beach empty, a thousand pirogues already over the curved horizon, nets long since strained by first catch. Noon bakes the seaweed on the strand and iodine and ozone crackle the air, till finally the waves far out start to gleam silver as the lowering sun cuts through the tumbling crests, and the afternoon heat haze refracts the color of the sun.

A first black dot bobs from over the horizon. Then another. Then a dozen. The race is joined. The beach market greedily awaits the first catch to be landed. The dots grow swiftly, but the wait is long. Sou'westers at last show their yellow, broad-bladed paddles flash in alternating four-man sweeps, the distance halves so that deepening troughs drop the pirogues from view, to pop up like released corks. The approaching trajectory intersects the descending rays of the sun till the boats and fishermen are but animated black silhouettes against the green and silver surface. Fifty yards offshore, paddles stay progress, and the pirogues turn parallel to the pounding surf. Wise eyes study the sea, then unsignaled shoulders hunch and paddles plow water as the prow is turned toward shore and muscle and wave hurtle it landward, a cockleshell caught in the crashing breakers that inexplicably, beautifully and skillfully glides into the lap of its wave and shoots upward to a scraping landing mid the curling foam.

Before the sharp-keeled boat can tip its catch into the surf, eight paddles are dropped and straining wet legs push the pirogue through the foam high enough on the beach not to be dragged out by the next wave. Women and children by the thousand throng around, children drag out the catch—four hundred pounds of fish per boat is not unusual—and their wives barter with the buyers. The crowd spreads to other boats arriving seconds later, some fishermen laboriously zigzag-drag the great pirogues up the beach to the high-water mark, others supervise the final haggling over the catch, the remainder spread the nets and lines in the dying sun.

Tons of fish spread on the beach from the thousand step-down-prowed, bright-painted pirogues that home here. Knives appear everywhere, and barracuda, captain, tuna and the others are cleaned, scaled or skinned on the spot. Some fishermen brand their share of the catch with unique and quickly identifiable slashes of knife into the tail, fins or head, a brand just as legal and as quickly attended to by violent justice as a cattle brand in America's West. Nearly every child in sight seems to have a large fish by its tail, either selling it or dragging it off home.

Two other villages, Joal and Fadiouth, first visited by the Portuguese in the fifteenth century, are inhabited by another kind of fisherman. These people are oyster eaters. They gather the oysters at low tide from the knees of mangrove trees in the swamps. Centuries of discarded shells lie everywhere, filling the land, spilling into the water, forming great mounds—some so old they now support hundred-year-old baobabs. Having subsisted for life on the oysters, these fishermen are even buried under their shells, in tunnels burrowed into the mounds. In Fadiouth, the only all-Christian village in Senegal, these shell graves are marked with crosses and sculptured wood.

But Senegal in centuries past looked away from the sea, east and north across the plains. Senegal was the western province of successive great Negro empires, empires whose lands today form several modern states.

The first of these, the Ghanaian Empire, was founded shortly before A.D. 300. The modern state that has adopted this name, Ghana, lies far to the south of the site of this ancient empire. An Arab scholar, El Bekri, recorded that Ghana's kings were able to field two hundred thousand warriors, forty thousand of them armed with bow and arrow. Gold was so abundant in the Ghanaian Empire that its free circulation was restricted in order to maintain values. This was accomplished by a royal fiat declaring nuggets to be cursed, gold dust being untainted and free for the use of all. The King, of course, was immune to such curses. One of the King's nuggets was large enough to be used as a hitching post for his horses.

Ghanaian legend claimed that the Empire's prosperity depended on a serpent deity, Ouagadou-Bida. Each year the most beautiful woman in the kingdom was sacrificed in the sacred grove to this god. One year, the sacrificial victim was defended by her lover. He cut the striking head from the giant serpent. A new head grew. Another cut, another head. Where each head rolled gold was later to be found. At the seventh stroke, Ouagadou-Bida the protective god was dead. The Ghanaian Empire died.

Ghana was succeeded by Mali, a new empire that conquered from the Sahara south to Nigeria and west to the Atlantic Coast. Mali eventually ruled an area larger than Western Europe—a Europe sunk in the Dark Ages of the fourteenth century, while cities of Mali, like Timbuktu, became centers of knowledge in many subjects such as astronomy, mathematics and successful medical operations. It was said at that time that books in the trade of Timbuktu brought a greater price than any other commodity.

In the first decade of the fourteenth century, Mansa Musa came to the throne of Mali. In his twenty-five years of rule Mansa conquered vast new territories with his hundred-thousand-man army, ten thousand of whom were mounted, innovated extensively in government and administration, and patronized education and the arts. But it was his wealth and largesse that spread his fame to the capitals of the world.

Being sincerely religious, in 1324 he set out on the Hajj, the pilgrimage to Mecca necessary at least once in the life of every true Moslem. The pilgrims, slaves and soldiers accompanying him formed a caravan of sixty thousand people. For expenses, Mansa Musa took a hundred camels, each packed with three hundred pounds of gold.

A contemporary Arab writer describes the emperor's visit to Cairo. Mansa Musa "spread upon Cairo the flood of his generosity: there was no person, officer of the court or holder of any office of the sultanate who did not receive a sum in gold from him. The people of Cairo earned incalculable sums from him, whether by buying and selling or by gifts. So much gold was current in Cairo that it ruined the value of money." An atlas compiled for King Charles V of France is decorated with a Negro monarch holding a scepter in one hand and a lump of gold in the other, and proclaims the Emperor of Mali "the richest and most noble king of all the land." It is no wonder that France offered a prize of ten thousand gold francs to the first European to find Timbuktu and return alive to tell about it, a prize collected in 1828 by a young Frenchman René Caillie who performed the prodigious feat disguised as an escaped Egyptian slave.

Ibn Battuta, the Berber born in Tangiers in 1304, spent much of his life traveling the Moslem world from Africa to China, and visited the Mali court a few years after Mansa Musa died. In his tale—a complete copy of his dictated memoirs was found in Algiers by occupying French in the 1830's—Ibn Battuta comments on the qualities of the people of Mali.

As "admirable qualities" he finds: "1. The small number of acts of injustice that one finds there; for the Negroes are of all peoples those who most abhor injustice. The sultan pardons no one who is guilty of it. 2. The complete and general safety one enjoys throughout the land. The traveler has no more reason than the man who stays at home to fear brigands, thieves or ravishers. 3. The blacks do not confiscate the goods of white men . . . They deposit them . . . until those who have a right to the goods . . . take possession. 4. They make their prayers punctually; they assiduously attend their meetings of the faithful, and punish their children if these should fail in this. . . . 5. They zealously learn the Koran by heart. Those children who are neglectful in this are put in chains until they have memorized the Koran . . . 'Will you not let them free?' 'Only when they know their Koran by heart.'

"But these people have some deplorable customs . . . 1. Women servants, slave women and young girls go about quite naked, not even concealing their sexual parts. . . . commanding officers . . . are served with food that is brought by women slaves, twenty or more of them who are completely naked. 2. Women go naked into the sultan's presence, too, without even a veil; his daughters also go about naked. On the twenty-seventh night of Ramadan I saw about a hundred women slaves coming out of the sultan's palace with food, and they were naked. Two daughters of the sultan were with them, and these had no veil either, although they had big breasts. 3. The blacks throw dust and cinders on their heads as a sign of good manners and respect. 4. And then a good number of Negroes eat the flesh of dogs and donkeys."

He writes of the emperor's audience on a raised platform that is "carpeted with silk and has cushions placed on it. [Over it] is raised the umbrella, which is a sort of pavilion made of silk, surmounted by a bird in gold, about the size of a falcon. The sultan comes out. . . . carrying a bow in his hand and a quiver on his back. On his head he has a golden skullcap, bound with a gold band that has narrow ends shaped like knives, more than a span in length . . . The sultan is preceded by his musicians . . . and behind him come three hundred armed slaves . . . Two saddled and bridled horses are brought, along with two goats, which they hold to serve as protection against the evil eye . . ." An imperial figure.

Today this great Empire is gone. In Senegal, descendants of its warriors are seen in every village market, at every feast and holiday. Their war-like nature survives in the national sport of Senegalese wrestling. A brutal, noble sport.

Only the physically elite participate—six foot four, two hundred and forty pounds. The entire village gathers for the contest. Tribal and village loyalties are vital, and each champion is backed by crowds of chanting, dancing, drumming partisans. The call of throbbing drums assembles everyone hours before the test of strength. Dancing societies weave and jerk in sweat-splattering celebration of the victory of their champion who is yet to fight. The competing roars multiply to a din that explodes when the fighters appear. Black masses of bulging muscles, they swagger up and down before the crowd in the expected parade of prowess, posing and flexing, escorted by frenetic drums and ecstatic singers hawking their herculean traits.

The fighters pointedly ignore each other, glancing everywhere but at the other. Mansa Musa's goat-guarded fear of the evil eye is palpable, a terrible menace yet. Each fighter's spell-caster goes to work, lighting small fires, burning foul-smelling concoctions of magic substances, gesturing mysteriously at the foe.

The drums drop silent. The fighters turn and for the first time that day gaze at each other. Flickering fingers fling curses and spells, suitably warded against by equally agile finger signals. An hour of this may pass before each is persuaded the gods are with him, and the wrestling match can commence.

Nothing, no hold, no blow, is barred. Anything goes till the opponent's back touches earth and victory is won. The test is great, failure before the tribe affects life in every aspect, defeat is oblivion, no effort to win is spared.

A bare fist flickers out, blood spurts from a slashed cheek. Again. A nose is crushed, and the flow carmines black chest. Bodies close with a rush, hands grapple for purchase on sweat-slippery arms, waists, legs. Heads butt. More blood. A hand closes fiercely on tight-bound testicles, and legs churn backwards to avoid the fall. A smashing elbow to ear loosens the grip. Another obtained, muscles bulge in slow, almost pantomime, grotesque effort. A straining of sinews, gladiators so equal it is painful. This equality dictates the length of the contest, an afternoon of struggle.

The end comes too suddenly, too quickly, an accident, an anticlimax. A hand snakes from nowhere and an ankle is captured, great muscles heave, scissoring legs frantically pedal backwards, to no avail. A flight, a crash of broad back to baked earth, victor spread-eagled across van-quished, the white dust a choking curtain to the act. The conqueror leaves on a chariot of exultant shoulders, his victim slinks away unseen through the crowd from the arena.

Once you have visited Africa, you never leave it. And Africa never leaves you. Its dust, mostly red, sometimes white, sometimes even black, settles on the heart, the soul, and remains forever. Even far away, the wind whispers. Yesterday at coppery noon it swept the Emperor's tanqua across Lake Tana, at twilight on Kilimanjaro it ruffled the mane of a hunting leopard, then capriciously swooped down from the Mountains of the Moon to swamp a pirogue, at midnight it wafted the stench of elephant to the pygmy in his jungle trench, this morning it sand-blinded a Kano-bound caravan, now it must be gone to stir the dust on another heart, and tomorrow—tomorrow it will look for you in Africa. The call is strong and insistent. One always answers. One always returns—if only in spirit.

FINIS